PLATO'S
CLOSET

PLATO'S CLOSET

Lawrence Giffin

ROOF BOOKS
NEW YORK

ISBN: 978-1-931824-65-1

Library of Congress Control Number: 2016933093

Author photo: Scott Waddell. "Hektor." 2008. Oil on linen.

This book is made possible, in part, by the
New York State Council on the Arts with the support of
Governor Andrew Cuomo and the New York State Legislature.

Roof Books
are published by
Segue Foundation
300 Bowery, New York, NY 10012
seguefoundation.com

Roof Books
are distributed by
Small Press Distribution
1341 Seventh Street
Berkeley, CA. 94710-1403
800-869-7553 or spdbooks.org

Contents

Let not thine eyes rove,
Peep not in corners; let thine eyes
Look straight before thee, as befits
The simplicity of Power.
And in thy closet carry state;
Filled with light, walk therein;
And, as a king
Would do no treason to his own empire,
So do not thou to thine.

Ralph Waldo Emerson, from "Gnothi Seauton"

Muse So Gray

I open the sodium ion channels and flood a nerve cell with
      sodium ions—
that's how I cause the membrane potential to become positive,
because at some positive membrane potential, I open the
      potassium ion
channels to allow the potassium ions to flow out of the cell.

Next I close the sodium ion channels to stop the inflow of
      positive charge,
but since the potassium ion channels are still open, I allow the
      outflow
of positive charge and the membrane potential plunges, bringing
      the membrane
potential back to its resting state, whereon I close the potassium
      ion channels.

I send the action potential down the length of the axon as a
      voltage spike,
increasing the membrane potential of one section of the axon,
then, increasing the membrane potential of the neighboring section,
      and so on.
In this manner, I proceed down the length of the axon until I
      reach the synapse.

Now I use the sodium-potassium pump to transport sodium out
      of the cell
and potassium into the cell so that I'm ready for the next action
      potential.

The Warlord Patroclus Addresses His Slave Girl Iphys

Spoil, you languish in the official residence,
your beauty the product of your desire to return
to a place whose allure is a function
of your subtraction from it,
so you remain to preserve it as such,
and only thus can you enjoy it,
gazing in its direction through
the facets of a bright crystal,
which alienate your wistfulness,
refracting and reflecting it
into a vision of home fulfilled.

It's the meaning of such a place I was after,
the spirit of it, when I first set out to claim it,
but even before then, it had to be put into a book,
which meant that those were not my deeds
recorded, so their meaning was always
that of my powerlessness to retrieve them.

A sediment of manners rolling across the seasons,
an overgrown footpath the graveyard spilled into,
these were just two things you could not bring with you.
The rest you refuse to name, or if you do, I do not understand.
It's possible the ineffable is what remains
ordinary enough to escape mention.

In its place, innumerable crystals
scattering the light. So many crystals.
The children bring you flowers
and trinkets that open and close, saying,
"Love's mysteries in souls do grow
But yet the body is his book."

These foreign elements that coincide with,
only insofar as they displace, the lost thing
(which is like a crystal in that it is as much as it is
such that it is part of no whole) become
another dumb book of poems wanting not to meet
the bookstore browser's gaze
but to organize the deluge around its alien spire,
to be irrefutable in its ridiculousness or if ignorable
to remain mildly irritating.

◊

Every encounter leaves a mark,
and the mark it makes is indelible,
even if its derivation is erased or if
it signifies nothing but a struggle
or skittish escape—breath on glass contracting,
the blue-green halo of a bruise—
because the fact of it all at once serves
as an index with no whence,
conducting one by force toward
an intention inferred in place of an
illegible abstinence anticipated in what
just seems to present itself as ordered rubble—
furtive motif—some refuse to remember. As luck
would have it, to be does not mean to have to be
forever, only to have to have been at all, which means
to be seated on one's own ass in the void.

Memory, categorical or curricular, finally
separates the memento from what meant more,
the accident from the cadaver, Adam's apple
from Fig Newton. Things leave one's hands,
even loved things, but they only ever fall into another's,
minused just from one's own small world,
and so it falls to what or who remains

to maintain, even against will, a ruin of memory
that threatens to disappear, forever collapsing in on itself,
over time becoming a lightless and ineradicable crumb
of a lightless and ineradicable crumb
that, adjacent to impressions, remains a crystal facet
so thin as to recommend a revised geometry
(or rather, a better geometer), the proofs of which are
worked out in a life lived as much out there as in here.

The mark of every new memory is added to this
ad-hoc ensemble—this *this*, which just is
the collective acknowledgement of its
withdrawn donation: clamorous propinquity
composed around a share—always just now
recognized—in a singular improvisation of time and place
that takes on the shape of the shape it happens to make.
It's name is a ceremony that prescribes
its own tradition, that is, it is a reenactment of
the prior surrender and the orchestration of its lament.
Each new recital the same and yet sounding
as if for the first time with whatever at all
having come before being recast as still one more form
in a chorus, a lossy cumulative number
like a hole at the bottom of the sea or
a crowd for its members to get lost in.

◊

When we descended on the barbarian village,
I did not know we were riding our way
into the pages of some book. I was there

for one thing, maybe two. Soon after we arrived,
it became clear that all this had happened before.
The patois. The retooled ruins. The illegible tinder.

When interrogated, their speech inexplicably
mimicked the *um*s of our *edictum* and *corrigendum*
as if some uncommitted memory sought

to disclose itself. Some local fetishes
of little value to us came wrapped
in ancient decrees and long-repealed statutes.

The seal had long decamped but its impression
remained on each act in decomposing wax,
imparting an inscrutable weight to each.

Some chronic condition severs an address from its
meaning so that what is called up is always a recall,
what is remembered is only its revocation.

The vacancy that once embraced what's gone,
which is as stubborn as a stone, is not lack
but lack's deficit of being, its unwelcome persistence.

In this way these people who would soon lose their customs,
their homes, their lives, were comforted by the knowledge
that these were never theirs in the first place.

They were now mine, and I knew I had
no choice but to enjoy them, privy
as I was to the vicissitudes of the season's yield.

I looked for your face in the faces
of cowering savages, as if I might find myself
there, too. Because it follows you.

It doesn't just stay behind in the place
that you left or left it. So you would have had to have
been there, too, if you were to have been at all.

◊

Restless reason in time resurfaces in memory
to cast in a facet its untimely aspiration,
which opens it and which it opens, since it is
the exaggerated gesture of what is and was not possible.

To affirm that loss, that is, to negate it,
is for one to become its steward, however forlorn,
however impossible or repugnant the task
of registering this whatever, this *this*, as the absolute,
that is, as the hatch marks of one's faults recopied
beneath the interdiction they inevitably spell out.

A voice comes to one in the dark, but always to one
unready, taken by surprised and so held in suspense,
                         breath baited as is the lamb led
into the fuzzy, suffocating silence of the abattoir.
Only when the call is repeated is one finally
evoked as such in timid and deferential reply,
in a voice that folds back on the first one
only now figured to be one's own, maybe not
all along but nevertheless now assumed—
a fold that maintains an inconcilable distance
between a thing and itself the breadth of the space
between a lamb's eyes.

◊

Of what's gone before remains this,
which never ceases dying, a wrenching
conservation. The fullness of its loss
is compensated by callous or gall.

Of what's left this has been overtaken—
the siren's alarm, the lone horse's crop-anxiety,

nicks in the walls of the abandoned city
where no one has lived for years.

Its chafing grit long gone,
the persistence of the mark seems to imply
a wish for its return, so much so
that some look for it everywhere,

wanting to know again what one
has never known as if for the first time.
That way, this can all have been
foretold in a book, the pure voice

of its ancient warning proving that this
is but an unrecognized repetition. Its purity
lets its meaning to become plastic,
irrefutable in the oblivion of its origin.

A sound inanity, an old standard, a classic—
what absorbs this remainder
in the universality that issues from
its meaninglessness, from the purity of its abstention?

The book closes just as easily as it opens,
buries as well as it divulges, and carved up
even with indices and paragraphs,
resists any use to which it is put. And so,

in its insistence, its initial silence
is met with the indifferent and thus
more patient and prehistoric silence
of its moss-like illegibility. Each word

remanded to the silence of none left
to recite it. Its meaning remaining
what meaning's left there. Oftener

a doorstop than telecom tech.

◊

Seeing you framed in that moment,
a wedge of time that spoke too faintly
of what had come before and what
might come yet. I could

in that moment address you,
standing beside my horse turning
only your face to me,
when some feeling had led you

absentmindedly to tug at
a tassel strung from my saddle
as if it were yours or were
to become yours—I could

in that moment plot only your place
and not your trajectory, could only trade
one for the other, stealing you into history
or leaving you to the unattested dust.

I knew I couldn't take it all with me.
My men and I would have to leave
most of it behind. And if you had stayed, if I
had left you behind, would I have had to

have left it with you? For years after,
would you have wondered
what *bellum* could have meant and why
I addressed you as such?

And if you had come, would it have remained,
or would we have lost it too in time

that metaphysical washer-dryer
with its transcendental settings.

A domestic obliviscence in which
the heat-affixed superhero decal on my
commemorative terra-cotta goblet fades
a little more each wash, now almost just

a white shape reminiscent of some
animal-oriented crime fighter.

And when I go, that shape will be
neither pure nor free, just irredeemable,
subject to chemical processes
as boring as they are difficult to explain.

A shapeless shape, unbelievably thin,
addressing its keyless cipher
to a vegetable cosmos. Darting
plaything I almost overlooked,
you were destined finally to be

so. And so, with every
metabolic process, for instance,
as my cells convert glucose into pyruvate,
I will universal death. Me, just

another knot in the inert,
a knot of knots,
industrial complex of quantum
suffering and forgetfulness.

◊

A slim volume seeks to account
for a discrepancy in the historical record,

and at first glance, it seems to have
accomplished its task. Now it remains

for someone to read it again, this time
more closely. And again. And closer still.
Until its surfaces begin to separate
in the air like loose leaves that come to rest

on boxwoods or in that little space
between the curb and the wheels
of traveling cars where everything ends up
eventually, taking on snow and meaning.

But if the book remained closed, the promise
would remain still, guiding equally
the weak and the strong, each yet-read page
another facet on the crystal of the book.

This book, stuck into your hands by choice or
by chance, it doesn't matter which, they all
look the same in the end, if only because
everyone's left or no one's left.

Whether it all exists to end up in a book
or its ending up thus only makes it seem so
doesn't matter. What's left, what's passed over,
is read as always having been since it's now all.

But now, for the time being, the book is read,
and read again for the first time in every reading.
Each is a chance or a choice not to be
again the reading that it was before.

And yet for each chance the book must
exist as that which is never finished,
only set down, in other words,

time is never exhausted, we are.

Your face, refracted by memory, appears
far from the one I want to see facing me.
And so in turning toward me
you seem only to look away.

And so I revolve within this crystal
palace, packed with those little baubles
that I couldn't toss out without also
finding myself alongside them on the curb.

And so turning, maybe I'll come
to recognize the crystal that I am,
the facet that lights another just so.

And if I were to shatter, I would be no more
or less myself. The moment would not arrive,
approaching as it does its unbelievable thinness.

◊

The crystal's absolute limpidity
is constructed of an infinite number
of scintillating refractions.

At each moment another cut
is added to the crystal's form
already crowded with facets—
each cut a moment of time
in space without depth.

The smallest cut that can be seen
is somewhere between the smallest cut
physically possible and the one unslit and uncut facet
that the figure of the universe

cuts in the minds of those fucking with it.

But the lapidary misery
choking on the diamond dust of collapsed facets
remains beyond both,

approaches the smoothness of a sphere
with the knowledge that an unvarying smoothness
is death or is at least the moment that would be,
if one could follow, immediately after death.
A microphotograph of a crystal

the billionth of a second before it is
obliterated by the violent light that illuminates it
becomes itself just one refraction
of a theoretical crystal across whose imperceptible facets
it passes unnoticed.

Shattering, it makes a kind of music. Shuddering,
the crystal's music is pure refrain,
the shape of its order the law of its shape.

◊

The book is just a set of coherent,
because incomplete, readings that
at each iteration add up to a
provisional entirety, which totalizes because

what the fuck else would it be so unruled,
each page a cryo-section protesting
denied access to the whole that takes
its time as a leaked inevitability.

Thus each reading assumes
the paranoid deflections of the last one,

must archive it shamefully
as the reading it couldn't become.

Not only to capitulate
but to give up entirely
on the morality that might
have justified one's resentment.

What's left is just
the operation of minusing plus
whatever residue written
to the register remains.

◊

What collapses is that immediacy
of sense, how the meaning of this or that
mark cut here or there is cradled,
conducted with such anxiety,
by the accidents that happened to have been
there then and that without grumbling
took on the burden of being themselves
unfinished and so grounded
on unstudied meaning but not in the sense
of debt, which happens to be
the gift of speech for those of us ensconced

now in our gratuitous dealings, or worse,
in the sense of the conservation of energy
as the law of cosmic indenture,
but in the sense of a debased ideal
that flattens difference only to find
it regrouping behind it, which positions
an infinite concern for anything at all
against the war of all against all
and its ethics of atomic differentiation.

Ever shrinking, each facet yet expands
this cruelly nonfatal exhaustion.

◊

All that's left is for the book to be
closed, it's reading a failure that ceases
to be nothing, that persists in niggling
irritation, which can only be alleviated
by the system that transcribes it to
another register, higher though no less
out of order.

It is all one insofar as it is alone. And all one,
independent and self-reliant, it is incapable
of being with you, to the point that this
incapacity takes on the quality of weakness
and forlorn will capitulate and abandon
its position, or (O! how the armor pinches)
it will mobilize to annex what ails it.

The soldier on his horse sees in the peasant
village only a generous inevitability,
exotic as limes and harried by
a lack of information, or rather a lack
of certainty about that on which this
ignorance alights—a vincible thing.

◊

Nothing ever really breaks down. The surfaceless glint off
anything keeps dying. I turned to look, but it was gone.
I put my hands together, but there was no sound.
I wanted to see myself between two mirrors
duplicated to infinity, but my head was always
in the way, and like you, I look with my head.

What kills you does not then die. What shuns you
affirms its undying devotion to you. Were you left
indefinitely to persist, it would counterfeit an analog
that could not have been.

◊

The book of so many pages exact as it is not
a word out of place, itself never finds its place,
its time, always ahead or behind, and so

contents itself by tagging any passing mode
that takes up its title with the seal of its censure,
the literal obliteration in a typeface vectorized.

    The book knows what gives up hides best
    and so remains only to be closed and replaced

    on one of those little metal shelves that organize
    loss and keep forgetting from being all at once.

And Others Who Are Mute Auditors:
a sequence for the guardians of the republic

I.

With what and with what tool will be
punctuated this question? Living now
as a vulgar and anonymous George Bailey,
himself already anonymous and vulgar,

yet absorbed in the task of having to
exist and to recover that existence
only finally to assent to it as it is,
now slightly displaced by the joy that extorts.

The question, The fuck? A honey that burns
the ear with the shame of having known
all along, having returned to the cave untanned,
shrugged and sat down now unbound in one's place.

Never to refrain, not even in the face of total
privation, must be what it's like to be a god.

II.

Beyond the light, the fact that there
could not have been another way for
the one you are, yourself less than
phosphorescent in glaucous universality,

it thrusts you into the care of those
better or better off than you,
traverses order's verdant term at an angle
bent by a history that undermines our chastity.

Not to tend the other that is finally
oneself but to attend it from whence
is to share in the play of captor and
slave, a flame that will not burn.

Another as she really is, neither exemplary
nor teachable, but a dressed address, deft and cleft.

III.

Already that corpse coursing to Camelot,
I fell in love with the land owner,
the hoplite, or at least, with the desire
to see (to see him see me seeing him astride).

To be seen and not to know was his
blight—gelded in grassy patrimony,
mine, a child for every hour of the day;
a necessary lie, a shining untruth.

What would require one to pull them
out into dumb sunlight? Askesis.
Zion. A need for recognition
of what in fact is.

The sun's severed rims, puckering apertures,
"Ye wretches, take your fill of the fair sight."

IV.

Our youths have been Hellenized to the point
that our alliance can no longer resist temptation
in the barracks, dispensing with the refrain
of our founding fathers to take up a spartan sex life.

Our father, whose overtakelessness coats
our arms in a shining sea green patina
and under whose absent eye anything is suspect
of corruption, his "wealth dazzles like the sun."

He says, Know thyself duped and kidded,
diddled and done, hoodwinked and suckered,
stiffed and shafted, fudged and gouged,
tricked, had over a barrel, and taken for a ride.

Looking away shall be my only negation.
"The duller eye may often see sooner than the keener."

V.

A lie is useless to the gods and useful
only as a medicine to men:
that one man can only do one thing well,
for we shall not want a panharmonic scale.

We must assume control over the narrators
of this class, expunge the verses, purge the State
of luxuries; just let one royal lie trickle down,
and judges will acquire a knowledge of virtue and vice.

Argument steals the hearts of one class,
and under the softer influences of pleasure
or the sterner influences of fear in Phrygian
mode, they will recognize and salute.

But now in that other place (as the poets say),
we have reason to be ashamed of the lie.

VI.

Necessary yet insufficient, to construct
what already is supposed to be:
The world cannot be a philosopher
if not already ordered.

The gods' useless lie is useful
as medicine for men, driven
by clear imperfection toward
ascensions crowning unyielding sky.

Is the public not the greatest Sophist,
especially when its word fails? When worlds
fall short of words, one must refrain.
All history occurs so to speak on credit.

Authentic philosophizing is powerless
within the sphere of matter-of-courseness.

VII.

We point to the idea as it emerges
from the other side of things, because
even we forget who placed it there
since so many bodies lie between.

White laurel of shriveled pleasures,
unreadily thrust by chance into
a trench whose latrine inverts
the naked and furious master,

her flanks flecked by beaded multiplications
of a world from itself in flight. Those
we threaten with disregard so as not to seem
hirelings might wander too widely

only to be told to "Tell them if you can."
And if they refuse to listen?

VIII.

Inasmuch as they are two, each is one
and need its contingency returned as harmony—
some other accounted and accountable for
the management of pancakes and preserves.

The nubs and knobs of girls and slaves,
of property, plicate the dispensation
of pleasures suspended from the earth's navel,
where the tangent's function zeroes out.

There a quiver equivocates the name of life,
whose work is death, word round which his lips close.
But now in that "other place" (as the poets say),
we have reason to be ashamed of the lie

and of they who in practice don't buy it but
who are not the same as those who can't afford it.

IX.

"The imitative poet who aims at being popular
is not by nature made, nor is his art intended,
but by the passionate and fitful temper,
which is easily imitated."

And yet, true poetry is a giantess
who straddles not the Hellespont
but who somersaults in skirts,
a crooked-footed skank who likes to watch.

Only in truth does the poet keep the lie,
affirming nothing, just as the claim made
by the poet-assassin of León turned on this brute obelus:
that the true lie is hated not only by the gods.

The gods belong to the field of the real;
the subject is there to find where it was.

X.

How to give full reign to the purgative effects
of this disease (rust of copper) without its truth
presenting the symptoms that authorize its absolute
nonrelation to the Good. A yield from the other

principle, which inclines us to recollection of our troubles
and to lamentation, and can never have enough of them—
with the slight difference that its impossibility is
induced to return, contra Lazarus, to that worn tomb.

If the exhaustion of its being in actuality is inverse
to that of the conditions that legitimate it, then the state
takes on a tragic beauty as when the hero dying
receives from the chorus the name of that fatal delusion

that hijacked his love and sense of duty
and so never dies, never finally fucking dies.

XI.

Finally to know and never again to be,
this is the curse of truth and why anyone
prefers to remain in despair and the fullness
of its meaning, its drama and pageantries.

Finally to know and never again to have is love's
fulfillment, its perfection in a gesture that can't be
recalled, a word as duplicitous as the lips
that conveyed it. The only mercy is that

the cave's mouth is now a wall of stone
barring return. Even an empty tomb,
however preferable, would be just
the revocation of the place of mourning.

All that's left is to mark the stone wall with
the idiotic mnemonic of generalized forgetting.

XII. Epilogue

And do you see, I said, men passing along the wall carrying all sorts of vessels, and statues and figures of animals made of wood and stone and various materials, which appear over the wall? Some of them are talking, others silent.

I sensed the Empire without seeing it, sensed a vast iron prison in which human slaves toiled. And I saw as if superimposed on the black metal walls of this huge prison certain rapidly scurrying figures in gray robes: enemies of the Empire and its tyranny, a remnant opposed to it.

But if the truth of the subject, even when he is in the position of master, does not reside in himself, but in an object that is, of its nature, concealed, to bring this object out into the light of day is really and truly the essence of comedy.

Iphys's Physis: A Closet Epic

No revolutionary canticle broke the mist
of that casque, and somewhere like a starry curtain
we drifted towards the Outer, where new myths
lay gasping at our white vanquished languor.

Frank O'Hara, from "Hatred"

Dedication: On First Looking into Halpern's *Porn*

My spirit's foreskin no longer holds what it don't
    know it knows or knew and had forgot, had had to have

known and not to've been or more like to've been
    without having to know or know why but learn how.

Like this, my spirit precedes me, Rob, is a play-worn G.I.
    Joe that as a kid I would command, *Back to the front!*

teeth tested and slid past the molars to scout
    the imperative's source, pushed farther

than I'd've liked and retched in joyful homecoming.
    What did he see, my die-cast grunt? *Benedictus,*

I had to beat it out of him, smearing him
    with truth serum till he coughed it up.

Before the will to know is first the dumb deed—
    an excrescence on the absolute that mistakes itself

for spirit, except that's exactly what spirit is:
    the arc of teeth marks on flesh reluctantly read

as cusses and slurs, a pretty turn of phrase suggestively
    vacuous, that is, what's visible without being exposed.

My spirit goes there for me, sees in my stead,
    is itself *ye wretches* exposed to the vision

take your fill, so that I maintain *of the fair
    sight!* my purity. My spirit is moved

by certain blots and smudges it encounters,
    which it assumes are addressed to it alone,

even though they are only the scuff marks of its own
    frantic searching, expecting the worst.

In this way, it always gets what it wants,
    finds the world's ill fit curiously fitting.

It's fickler with what evidence it doesn't leave behind, has
    preferences, predilections, is discerning, opinionated,

starts to see constellations burnt on its toast;
    it comes and goes, is housed wherever it wills,

shifts residence from beasts to men, from men to beasts,
    but always it keeps on living. All things are fluent;

every image forms, wandering through change,
    but spirit is evermore the same,

though passing always to ever-changing bodies,
    and in this way, what was never there suddenly

was there all along, and when it has found
    such a kindred spirit in the flesh (and what is

an image if not flesh?), it goes out into
    the image's never-made promise of happiness,

which my spirit gladly hears regardless, in fact
    donates that promise in all its sovereign naiveté

and is thus the bone that falls from its chalky heights
    and bottoms out, taking by the very same gesture

with which it gives, and anticipating imminent
    pleasure, deathly so, my spirit enters the pornstar's image.

The camera all but disappears. "I am the camera now,"
    she says, "pointed at the back of my mind

"I am the tripod upon which for now
    turns the world but which never turns;

"I am the colorless lens and thus blindly looking
    when I don't show and showing when I look away."

In this glancing structure of transubstantiation, when
    my spirit occupies the image it longs to look upon,

coinciding to a hair with *the* figure, I am more
    and more divested, increasingly threadbare in donation,

until the moment I perceive I risk a decadence beyond
    enjoyment, such that the next moment I may become

irredeemable, one grain shy of a heap. At this point,
    jerking it in one clean motion, I pull back on my spirit,

saving it from total dissemination in this pink star.
    It's that quick, the movement of the spirit,

but its return is decisive. Having retrieved it
    from the flesh of the image, and this is key,

if I wipe it off it in anticipation of the next
    investment, then that is the height of pornography.

Were I instead to pop it in my mouth and suck it
    clean—that's something altogether different.

Spirit is truth's shadow, that is, it writhes in dirt.
    It's not the prison of the body, but its got-told top.

It's not against the half-breeds running riot and is
    in fact their bad speech in unison echoing off

the soon-to-be déclassé. It's important here to be clear,
    spirit is not an illusion, a stopgap, a *Fight Club* poster

pasted over a hole in Being. Spirit is the fucking hole,
    is the hole's quarterly self-evaluation.

Spirit gets up in front of the village and castigates
    itself for intellectual crimes against the Party.

Spirit wants to see, wants to stick its face
    through the hole and motorboat the void.

Spirit wants only to spear it with its bowsprit
    and to double its pleasure with a refreshing stick

of spearmint gum, to sit on it and spin on it, to spit
    on it and pin it like a beetle on cork-backed felt.

This is not meant to be a defense of necessity by way
    of the backdoor—being the only possible world,

this one's the best, no contest. It's just that
    it's no longer useful to appeal to ends; the ends'll be all,

"Fuck this shit," and split. Worse, they might actually *fuck*
    this shit, and if that shit is us, well, you'll know the drill—

But before that, we gotta get this epic started,
    this belted strain, six-fingered duke, a number

scored by a ghillie-suited Chanticleer, his makeshift
    ditty bag an extemporaneous scat, a roadside busk

bursting on the way to Damascus. Paid out in poets'
    severed members, he strums on his busted lute

a plaint of lusted booty lost and a laureate post busted
    to Pfc, another swab on the clock with a crusty mop

squeezing out a slop of bleach and reproductive overkill,
    inured through constant exposure and by a deep familiarity

with the mechanics of the whole thing. What—
    did you think this roll of TP put itself in the booth?

And who do you think cleans the decks' heads
    and polishes the door's knobs? Does it not matter?

The hankering that drives pervs here is for
    a One who's wager is a skeptic's protective *epokhé*.

Is it pornographic, Bob, your utopia? Is all reification obscene?
    Obscene in its ineffable unscrewableness, such that edging in

the French mode is all in how how one withholds *le dernier
mot*, which hinges on one's preference: Bataille or Blanchot?

How swiftly down the dream you do run
    with all the Bayers in and out of tune in tow:

the kool *poetes* moe dee denouncing
    themselves in exonerating versification,

completing Bey's radical project with two left orthopedics
    or translating Kanye's Marxian xenoglossolalia

with the French fries of pale boogie, faces
    cute enough to blush or bruise bluish, strolling

leisurely with Baudelaire and Debord
    tucked under an arm, their pervert verses

preserved in ivy-green graffitoed grottoes. What
    an honor it must be to be the instrument by which

global capital enjoys itself, the writing imp-
    lement with which it critiques its own decadence,

yet blessed with a guilt that never
    winces the soldier but which whittles

the comrade with her own penknife
    because her every word articulates the totality.

But you, Rob, in your widening panegyric,
    like a hawk encumbered with his hood

explaining metaphysics to the nation,
    I wish you would explain your explanation.

It's hard to tell if your hubris is planned
    obsolescence or just a sign of your wish

to supersede all warblers here below. Your porn
    shows too much flesh and not enough skin.

I can't bop to its jam, Bob; I can't bob to its
    dub, Rob. "The well is drye that should refresh."

Your porn abstracts like an intel spider
    in the fields and cells of my body in state,

logjam of snatched residue rubbed off in transaction,
    crawled by a virgin's dual-use algorithm.

Screening coarse data, you mask a lily-like hypervigilance.
    Think you not its thought a bit dry, Bob?

No, you seem to insist on the authenticity of jargon,
    thinking you can wring out its congealed labor

in a tortuous prosody and convey it frictionless
    through the ghost words of departed hippies.

You've got a depth only an interrogator could love—
    and all porn is proof against salvific depth.

The referent collateralized against a gonzo
    autocritique, the still spit on which it spins, only

appears because it stands between us and its own
    (more monstrous and toxic) conditions. Whether

wellspring of utopian longing, collusion of the stars
    behind the firmament's totality (yr *topos koinos*),

or spiderhole for disillusioned regroupment, the conclusion
    drawn from unassailable premises is necessarily terror—

God from his safehouse conducting the affairs
    of mortals by his very abstention (abstraction?).

Running frantic, we here below ask,
    "Is this what he wants? Is this it? This?"

But all these years, without anything close
    to a decent model of the Ideal or any

reasonable articulation of a logical imperative
    operating at the heart of our nature, wherever

that is, we seemed to have functioned with some success
    and if anything have refined our notion of ethics as calculation,

returning it to its radical, the third person reflexive.
    What did the moderns bequeath us if not a belief

in the impotence of nature or at least in its indifference
    to its own imperative? That's why monsters are without

reflection, the *is* of what *should not be*: the definition
    of 'accident.' (The recidivist commodity is still not

equal to commodified recidivism.)
    And the future? It can't be anything

but the promotion of the narcissism
    of minor differences to the level of policy.

"Whither porn?" you ask. My question then will be,
    "Whence?" From whence will it have issued

bearing across its cheek the pink welt
    of its origin in the heart of our natures?

For you it's when the market is aestheticized.
    When all that is is visible, and all that is visible is,

when you're dangled from what you dangle, when
    what advances withdraws, when what issues hoards

(and the longer I linger in your war porn, the more
    am I convinced this definition supersedes all others).

But to drag it out into the light of day, for me,
    is to plant in it the flag of your own dirty drawers.

St. Paul wrote, If not for the Law, how would
    I know I sin? Shame is the fruit's bitter sweetness,

the butthole's wince. Take a hint from the old mole
    working his wad in the dark of Plato's Closet.

You've had your shot, now it's his turn
    to skate the icing and upload his GoPro gonzo,

category-less (neither ebony nor asian, gay nor lesbian)
    and thus indistinguishable from the *horror of everydayness.*

In Plato's Closet, there is a screen in front,
    a slot to the right of it as long as a dollar is wide,

a chair in front of them, and to the left and right
    of that, two oblong holes cut through each wall

about three feet off the floor. Indeed, you see,
    in Plato's Closet, truth runs crosswise to art.

I invite you to enter this hole that leads neither in nor out
    but is just the temporal pleasure of articulation,

of passing, and once inside to close the door and with dirty
    hands deposit your wad in the glowing slot

and enjoy my first pass at demoralizing repulsion
    as antidote to the mobilization of my desire—

always a gloryhole can become a backdoor to escape
    the circulation of the already inexchangeable, the immune.

Spirit, man, I'm talking about fucking spirit,
        what Dana called "an effable thing." What is

obscenity but that the sign itself against
        my will realizes my value? Without protest,

the *locum* takes the warm purchase right in the puss,
        and I am pegged to a mystical standard, absolved

by credits or Apollo's timely chariot. What we
        center on distracts. A fragment of poetry appears

whole by virtue of its isolation. By the fact of its
        utterance, the monologue of poetry seems to tell all,

an aspect precluded by dialogical prose,
        which obscures its own totalizing will under

an economic form of justice. The poem tends toward
        autonomy simply by an illegitimate assumption of it.

And this is its one virtue in vice, that in the midst
        of telling all it includes the status of its delusion.

As much looter as lieutenant, it does not pretend to the
        prosaic delusions that are the describable conditions

of setting, scene, and motive, enabling endlessly deferred
        action while a committee is formed to study the issue.

And so, without the same expectation of prose
        continually to leak information as promising as it is

strategically inconclusive, poetry is free to indulge
        in idiosyncratic diction, in obscenities and epithets.

Where prose makes explicit what was never there to begin
  with, poetry struggles to distract from what is

most disappointing about hidden truth—its revelation—
  to obstruct a meaning that if said outright would seem

banal, thus, to dodge banality by intimating some
  seductive something else, something not yet arrived,

something yet to be seen. Is this poetry or pornography?
  Or is pornography rather the pretense of disclosure,

oversold revelation, stretched out against the sky
  like a heretic theorized upon the rack?

Can we even conjure up today a depth
  that would merit such medieval tending?

Take, for instance, the porn theater patron
  and his vigilance, which in the light of day

drives speculative reason to flash
  back into that same darkness cut

only by the repetitive flicker—the world is worse for his
  obsolescence. It's the function of meaning to be this right

here in front of you but also not this, no, something
  better that this has gotten in the way of. Is porn then

the opposite of poetry: the fullness of an instant?
  Is porn the cynical citation of what's visible, sayable?

And is poetry then a mystical ecstasy,
  archorite's arcana, or guild's mystery

the initiate manifests in an epiphanic masterwork?
    I guess it depends on what your definition of 'is' is.

Poetic diction, however obscene, is antiporno-
    graphic to the extent that it precludes any other way

of saying the same thing, eschewing the deference
    of narrative for a form of speech promulgated

on its mystical immediacy and universality
    to make up for what eludes us in our everyday.

Oh, but this is all too explicit, too straight. In silence and
    alone, in an attitude reminiscent of right prayer,

men read about women that circulate. The whorehouse
    sits in the space between work and home. The hooker

moseys on the borders of the industrial district.
    The strip club is near the airport. Sites, to put words

in your mouth, you could call the "subcommons
    of immediacy." (I just coined that, but I'd be willing to trade.)

I haven't even touched on those who keep their porn secret,
    who let its effects meet the world in their red-eyed squint,

their open leer, hocked cuss worming its way
    into the ears of those who say it with diamonds

and mop the brows of their loved ones with hundreds,
    stuffing the yellow polka-dot bikinis of the disappeared

with singles (automatically, the brown rental
    resumes a spirit of gratitude when,

hide tanned for outgrowing her britches,
    a fault switch installed in her at the border raises

the counterfactual of subsisting instead on cum
    dredged from Toshiba crystals or of her returning

these rare metals mined years ago just down
    the road back to the earth through shortened breath.

Strange flowers these plumes of capital). I don't want
    to discourage you from writing your porn.

We all strive for a well-balanced graphology,
    a slurred spook, a pneumatic purr. But some

things can never be brought into the light of day
    without leaving behind the very aspect that made them

appear worth exposing. A privilege is never revoked
    simply for being such. Its unevenness is not a fault

but fully its intention. In the end, it's just you
    looking back from the mouth of the cave, saying,

"Can't you see? Can't you see the truth? It's right
    in front of you." But in reality it's just you

standing there with your dick in your hand.
    Is that what you're referring to?

In this way, our dirty thoughts are no different
    from dreams: secreting meaning but boring recounted.

Just as a dream when recounted loses
    the significance of its immediacy and

the immediacy of its significance, the object
of one's desire can only appear to another

as something ridiculous if not disgusting—
offensive, even. What is curious, finally,

is the compulsion to reproduce the beloved object
in speech. The need for recognition can be overpowering,

but it's risky and often ends badly,
as when first having failed to obtain confirmation,

the lover describing his beloved to a skeptical other
then begins to augment or tailor their description,

working under the assumption that he had been
too vague at first or had chosen the wrong words.

After subsequent failed attempts, the lover considers
whether the fault lies either with his interlocutor

or—*O! the horror*—with the object itself,
and it is at this point that the lover decides

only aggression toward this other can save the beloved
object from the scorn implied in the other's indifference.

In all this, what the lover has failed to realize is
that he has already betrayed the object of his desire.

In his struggle to represent the object
to another with recourse to an external medium,

language in this case, he divests the object
of the very aspect that gives it its power,

an aspect he anxiously tries to redress
    by exposing the beloved to the judgment

of another, that is, its singularity.
    In the unconditional immediacy

of its allure, the object had appeared
    to him as something arbitrary. And he

makes the all-too-common mistake of believing
    that a third-party appraisal would confirm its worth.

The goal instead: to sustain desire of the beloved,
    to don the masks that animate them, and to do so

without recourse to meaning or reason.
    The petulance of one's love is sufficient

to bestow glory even on foolishness and errancy
    ("There is no disgrace in a noble pursuit deceived").

Infinitely debased, the lover can never lose,
    is ennobled by their foolishness. The poem,

similarly, anonymizes fascination
    and elevates one's hideous pathology into

a bounteous symbol suppressing any
    relation that exists between it and its beholder.

Even the small distance that a poem insinuates
    by its very structure between speaker and

subject creates sufficient ambiguity
    to cause the fetish to shed its particularity

and take on the form of an enigma
    whose beauty affects more deeply than others

the one who wonders what others see in it, whose
    exultation and transports of delight are merely

his or her incomprehension as to why.
    It is beautiful simply because it is on display.

By choosing the form of the poem, the poet can
    indulge in pillow talk under the guise of universal address,

and by means of this strange logic, we can affirm that
    the most artificial poem is also the most confessional.

This is not to say that you should stop writing
    your poem-porn, Rob, or that you should fill it

with a few important words, and a lot
    of low-keyed, dull-sounding ones.

It's necessary to have it down on paper.
    A person without a clear and honest sense

of their shameful thoughts is a turd. So fill your diary
    with trash and filth and smut. I promise you'll find

realized there a distinction, until now only ideal,
    between politeness and politics, between policy and license.

It's about training your trainer and being your own
    bossy bottom. It's about getting exactly what you want.

You've earned it, this authentic replica of the totality
    with twenty different vibration settings. Do it. Be the thing,

be the very fucking thing you were
　　meant to be. Not you, Rob, I'm addressing

everyone leash in hand, hanging each one's
　　ownmost stainless and hypoallergenic cranial acorn.

I know it sounds crazy, but you'll just have to trust me.
　　It may work in practice, but it doesn't work in theory.

Reading your *Porn,* I can tell it wants
　　only to disappear. It wants not to exist and is

simply the consequence of its struggle
　　to manifest its revocation and nothing more.

And yes, that is the very mark of beauty,
　　the blemish that saves us from the ideal *fleur,*

so to further mar your *confessio amantis,* I pimp
　　this coy missive, tight lipped and suggestive, bound

and passed around, a rich promise with nothing
　　to back it up, a toxic asset repackaged as a drag epic,

crotch rock that should be sung with the barrel
　　of an M9 locked between the teeth, a femural dirge

that would be the Hegelian equivalent of
　　a timarchic *yawp* sounded over the ruptured

pipes of a church organ from the bashed trachea
　　of Byron's cornelian canter—its noise, unintelligible,

still registers as sound, as what yet may come
　　to be regarded as speech, literal in its near silence,

audible behind the marble statuary when, in solitude,
    against the round walls of the pantheon you lean

hearing instead a whisper that crawled
    up the dome years ago, out through

the blood-red oculus to wiggle blindly
    across the surface of the planet finally again

to enter, only this time on the far lip of the
    sun-filled *œil de boeuf* and back down

the dome's long-repainted surface to mark
    its make in your ear as if in confidence.

For all you know, it's the bloody gurgle
    of a gibbetted godhead spouting gibberish,

a carnelian hash red like Manhattan
    clam chowder from the busted mouth of Moses.

So, you know it's all in good fun and, in a sense,
    just my final project to get me out from under your

tutorship, undeserved and unasked for and so an errant
    philos, in the name of a generous invitation

to a common cause ever unnamed,
    which you lent me having read my gifted

Burning Plane and *Jacket* crack at erudition,
    and writing in '09 to thank me and mail me *Weak Link*.

A banner day then when a poor *eromenos*
    tops his unpaid *erastes* (Author! Author!), but IRL,

you're no Laius and I no Oedipus, just two
    masterless hammers banging away at the quays,

in the same spot but decades apart,
    your combat zone giving way to my driving

range, your mag stack surpassed by my
    cascade of windows, across which is glimpsed,

reversed in reflection, your epigone nearing
    his apogee, guilding his lily in the historic genre

to matriculate *ungh!* into the Academy,
    whose password is raised on the pike of its own

impossibility, that of pure negation,
    which would separate the past altogether

from the present, and repudiate the inertia
    of a storied guilt whose unsolicited advances

my widest kin seems only able
    to parlay into irony or rampage,

a life of *what ifs* and gray rape or
    a blaze of glory built upon a foundation

of free porn and the entitlements
    it assumes on one's behalf.

One doesn't have to go to Kandahar to see
    the politicization of dopamine, the instrumentalization

of what might be a base and ineradicable aggression,
    what Lacan called the "armor of an alienating identity."

What does porn give man if not the "total form
        "of his body" *du jour,* a two-way mirror that is

the facial agnosia of an underdeveloped ego,
        giving knowledge its final paranoiac structure.

It's how you can "get off knowing,"
        which underlines your question, "What happens, then,

"when the thing we need to see [ye wretches]
        in order to know ourselves *no metaphor*

"nor parable is a corpse *strong meat*
        of simple truth [take your fill] withdrawn

"from view [of the fair sight]?" What if it turns out
        this corpse withdrawn is that of a female soldier

(or even of a male soldier turned female)?
        But a female soldier would be impossible;

the substrate never appears as such,
        the thingy itself, the view from nowhere,

the horror of nothing to see, "lost
        in the vessel of exchangeable options."

But shame would keep you from writing it,
        shame that others might laugh to find you

actually thought you might be *that,* an effable thing.
        Or is that just me? Either way, the poem's task

is to measure that difference.
        Read thyself in the report, the free porn.

Turn the page, click NEXT, swipe left—
    next line, next pic, next vid might be

just that orthopedic vision in which
    you would finally recognize yourself.

Let my poem be your poem's beard, naive as young
    Tiresias, "on whose cheek the down was just darkening,"

when his sight was revoked, and let it begin with
    the following note on pederasty and naturalization:

In pederasty, the erotic relation was secured
    against the feminine and its erotic frenzy

in the form of archaic Bacchantes, bad citizens
    with their love of penetration (and what is

penetration but the blindness to my insight,
    omen to my downy owl, *mensa* to my *libro*,

seeing as how we are two men so unladylike
    in address?). It was the *eromenos*, the schoolboy,

who risked *atimos*, dishonor, in his passivity.
    Ravished by those to whom he was entrusted,

his rape was justified as the consequence
    of his dronelike desire to be penetrated.

Erotic love is nothing if it is not
    the labor of initiation creating a closed

community without excess. For Plato,
    music is excessive and effeminizing;

it makes men soft *(malakoteroi* or *anandros)*,
    and only when the flautists (the *auletrides)*

and the floutists (the *pornoi)* are dismissed
    can the symposium on erotic love begin in earnest.

(And yet he spends his final hours
    getting in touch with his feminine side.)

The "unmastered remains" you hope to stimulate
    in order to free yourself from the porn of war

may be those of a woman, one turned out from
    the Symposium only to be raped with a tire iron.

Pederasty made the continuation of the political order
    a matter of shared trauma (since rape is always taken

to be an isolated incident), a trauma circulated, passed around,
    one that no one can or wants to claim, i.e., the *munus,*

the gift of sight. The *eromenos* was always extorted into
    citizenship, into a society built on a whispered tradition,

its *mysterium* passed down mouth to mouth,
    like a word made flesh, fraternal order forged

through shared humiliation mastered
    by its infliction on another in turn,

an order in which the abject and the subject
    coincided, where one accepts this humiliation

with the guaranty that one day he would be able
    to wield the paddle in turn. This system of succession

was core to the Greek system of democracy, but the soldier
   who defended this democracy is the *phaule auletris*,

the poor pro, cheap and easy, null device to which
   is written the pain of the powerlessness to master that pain.

The *eromenos*, beloved pupil, cum ringing in his nose,
   ringing his hypothalamus to extort a little ass play,

the riot cop pressing his warm *regula* to the unruly puss
   of some already-speared spoil who couldn't stand

to spare some acrid valor, told to nut up and strip down,
   like son, like father (fruity *pharmakos* aching for a few

souvenir brazil nuts, hepcat swinging by his tail
   with the caption, "Hang in there!" printed

on the back of the postcard where is signed over to me
   in absolute privilege a value vested against the black

standard of the gold coast), or precarious *metoikos*
   constantly menaced with sharecropping or a switch

even an olive branch can't rival: Their divestiture
   is spun as our lack (of which there is no such thing),

something remediable through tutelary subjection,
   birthright or prospect, a good subject to duty

(the choice of voluntary servitude having always been
   a free choice made for me, before me, by me on my behalf,

a choice made before I was able and for which
   I am always responsible and so potentiates volition),

above all as the freedom not to choose, not forced to
 choose and, forced not to choose, *les vouloir perpétuer.*

How is an *eromenos* ever to master himself
 when his value is that of an object of desire?

The *kinaidos* was conceived as 'a man socially deviant
 in his entire being, principally observable

in behavior that flagrantly violated or contravened
 the dominant social definition of masculinity',

the latter often represented as fulfilled in the future
 of the (ideal) hoplite. The outlander, the totally fucked,

the *atimos kinaidos,* is a female soldier who has
 forgotten how to die. Only when she finally looks down

at the corpse that she is, at the wound through
 which her spirit escapes, homoerotic aporia where

her cock used to stand at attention, does she then
 fall out. Is utopia masculine, waiting as it does

for the gesture to find its completion
 in an honorable discharge, a legal consummation?

What about the future of a drag queen in fatigues?
 A poet mimicking a philosopher? (Is a philosopher just

a sophist tucking?) On the hook for the last political gaff
 (a Nazi-themed Brazilian sex tape), Socrates, wanting

these republicans perpetuated, put to the city in speech
 its self abuse or, to quote some frog prince, "poetry

"exhausts itself in search of the nothing,
    and this is what renders poetry complicit with death."

And by reliving this abuse of language,
    playing general to a cell's third bed,

do your findings become idiotic,
    or is the personal still the political?

What do you think are these *disjecta membra*
    you're grasping at, Rob, as if by touch's false

immediacy you might find what's yours
    in the hardwiring of auto-affection,

an immediate mediation where self-mastery
    is identical to self-pacification?

Take care not to find there only the need to know
    oneself, a circuit describing the circumference

of a collapsing star. For instance, what my john gets
    was his to begin with—a vision, a touch, a transaction

simply grants him permission to check that box.
    Sometimes he chokes me near death, and others,

I brain him with an ashtray
    and pocket what e'er he's got on him.

But these are no more real, no more autonomous
    (like Skynet), than the clear nymphs of desire.

If I brush back the lock that falls in his face,
    I am not his mother, and yet his wistfulness

completes its circuit, and he cuts a maternal
    swath from the endless stream of intensities

that bathe his inputs constantly. His anonymous
    cock convulsing in my ass takes nothing from me.

Its anonymity is not the result of my ignorance
    or of his disinformation or propaganda. It's d.b.a. is

simply withheld, as is mine, and in the gap
    opened up by that abstinence a multitude

of needs are met and no debt incurred. Everyone
    walks away happy and no one had to quote Locke.

And if God is involved in everything, whether
    as a Calvinist or Emersonian, it means God is

the ecstatic dick or the unmistakably female corpse,
    and since he's not, there's no tally to fudge.

It may be my problem alone, but I don't want to live
    in a universe with spooky action at a distance.

Your theory of mediation dreams a frictionless lube,
    a noiseless channel, gorge sans gag, where brushing back

a lock of hair would be a monstrous abbreviation
    summarizing the entire sequence from the big bang

to the Trans-Pacific Partnership, but there is
    a kind of mercifully incomplete anamnesis

built in to the universe (though it's actually not
    "built in" but is the inexpedient condition

of why there's anything at all), and since energy
    can neither be created nor destroyed, sublimation

owes no fidelity to the former purity of the now-
    modified impulse—the trade corrupts absolutely.

The commodity does not say the all of its value.
    Every point of articulation is a weak link. Reviewing

her own autopsy report, the soldier says, "That's not
    "my wound." And while no less real, it is yet not hers.

That difference is not slight, no matter
    the masses mobilized based on the findings:

Even the shortest distance between the wound
    and the report that exhausts its informational content

is yet infinite. This distance is that same gap,
    the gap the present makes within the inevitability

of the future, between entering and exiting the toilet
    at the Prince Street stop on one's way home from work.

In these moments of transaction or translation,
    of transubstantiation, total exchange is impossible.

Even in death, something of the body does not
    become property of the state, is not represented,

nothing in itself, but only the incompleteness
    of any representation, its POV and vanishing point.

What of the body does not become the property
    of the state is the body of the state. Unremarkable.

But I think that's maybe what you're getting at, as well,
    but from the other side so that the state appears as some

mythical lucky Pierre, the joy of middle management or
    the infrathin overlap of patiency and agency ("Physician,

heal thyself!"). Now let me venture a thought, and this
    isn't addressed to you personally, Rob, but to all of us

who search for utopia not in the ecstatic
    or kairotic time of the orgasm and the encounter

or in the vagrant temple circumscribed by a leer
    or a lean but instead in the pained and meticulous

construction of contretemps in the everyday,
    of which the poem is one possible mode—

so that, for instance, valorizing neither immediacy
    nor dailiness, the lived instants of O'Hara are

subordinated to the everyday (I do this. I do that.)
    in such a way that the banality of what is (and thus

of his perception of it) is not (for lack of imagination)
    taken for the exceptional quality of being anything at all

but is made free and eternal in a work
    assiduously tended to and labored over

as is a garden continually balanced
    on the intersections of its threats

or a song on the fine thread drawn between the
    austerity of its score and the surfeit of its performance.

In my Academy garden, which is not unlike Olive
        Garden, when e're a worm is derosed, a rose is surplused.

At its center a plane tree, arboreal emblem
        of my absolute desertion, unrepentant annihilating

will of my privilege. Come, Rob, go AWOL with me
        and rest in the shade of my epic, while I read you

it. It's got crude and sexual humor, a comic
        violent image, and some drug references;

sequences of terror and violence and some
        sensuality; pervasive strong brutal violence

and terror; brief nudity, strong bloody violence,
        some graphic sexual content, crude humor,

suggestive content, and swashbuckling action;
        adventure violence and scary images; intense

sequences of action/adventure violence, including
        frightening images, epic battle action, strong violence,

and gore; intense disturbing situations
        and brief drug use; scenes of surgery;

mild rude humor and some peril; mild suggestive
        humor, some innuendo, some teen partying, and a fight;

sexual references, drug and alcohol use, sexual content,
        smoking, and brief strong language—all involving teens;

some suggestive dancing, strong brutality and grisly
        violence; brief sensuality, some mild action, and gore,

violence, criminality, sensuality, and crude language—
    again, all involving teens. Now, doesn't that sound like

a tale worth waiting through the previews for,
    and what is this preamble if not the obnoxious

overtures of a lowdown, drunken *dériveur*
    flashing his brights into the fragrant azaleas

of Overton Park, and who spitting out an epithet
    coats an anonymous cock (to love the sinner

but hate the sin). What pleasure parts the drool-
    encrusted lips of *your* totality? For me, it's a tactical

dopiness that succeeding concedes
    and, dealing sealed lips a blown kiss

missed and planted in air, is flushed at its
    brash and barely concealed verdancy.

In this and in all things, your porn
    is always one step ahead of mine

(though, again, there is no disgrace in a noble
    pursuit deceived), its sandals printing *akolouthei*,

"follow me," on the dusty paths of some well-
    rutted heath. Its timbre always receding. Thus

abandoned, dare I tarry and demand my time
    in the sun, my leer but a squint in uncaved sunlight?

Chorus

Some dedication, huh? Reading it, you'd think the author had a real bone to pick with this Rob. But it reads like some pigeon-chested chest thumping, right? So why keep on pretending? Why continue to play the lover, the scholar, the tease when played so unconvincingly? Simply because it is found between the covers of some book, should one therefore presume the poem has been denuded of its artifice? It strips down to nothing, nothing at all. (There is no *there* there.) In the early stages of its composition, before even the semblance of a form had dawned suddenly like a tragic *anagnorisis,* the poem was barely a skeleton of ribald puns and nonsense wordplay overwrought to the point of bastardy. But randomly from this primordial void sprung the phrase, "regular Regulator," which immediately brought to the mind of the author Warren G's single "Regulate" featuring Nate Dogg. It was the narrative of this song that introduced into the nascent formlessness of the poem questions surrounding masculine homosocial bonding in the shared denigration of women, primarily in the proximity in male fantasy of violence and sex (after all, after gunning down several men, Nate Dogg switches his mind "back into freak mode").

The relationship of Nate Dogg to Warren G seemed to echo that between Patroclus and Achilles, though due to his ignorance of classical texts, the author made Achilles (here styled "Killa Beez," a reference to the similarly named UAV) the superior of (Project) Patroclus. The song provided the kernel on which to build a poetic interrogation into how men police masculinity, how they discipline masculine heterosexual desire into its current historical form—with all its anxieties of potency and its attendant acting out against women—which is why Killa Beez rails against Lysistrata (the "army disbander"), who maintains an exclusive disjunction between war and sex.

Of course, to compose the impotence of white masculinity as a poem is to point to, without indicating, the space between the mask and the face of the actor donning it. And of course, you came here not to see him or even to see that which he portrays. Before anything else, you are here for this noncoincidence. The chorus explains nothing; we can only remind you of the unreality of both actor and character, which we think has some significant political value.

I.

Like all epics, this one begins with a child,
    in this case, me, being buttfucked by his father

in blackface, a schoolyard littered in klanprop,
    and the bombast from the swelled muzzle

of a la-di-da CSO who's hypoxiating stars-and-bars-
    emblazoned sash flatters the gravelly ballasts

of his sunken head, so that this haughty
    donkey fancies himself a regular Regulator,

knuckles inked *para bellum,* coined street-Greek
    for a biscuit branded *SPQR,* sump plug

for Roman holiday; his cloacic cognomen,
    a romaji *gulp*, staged occasion for friendly fire

turning on this spit/swallow obelisque. His astigmatic
    mistake—meaning, he can't have it all at once—

is not checked by *la fantasme génétique,* having
    thoroughly sublimated any vacillation into a vassalage

to his distressed *midons* whose dental abolition
    in offering his off and fay bung to a supreme camp

chaplain (some *gentes* to pluck his molluskan ianthe),
    is the learner's permit, an invitation to sit as the guest

of honor, the center of encyclopedic *misteres,*
    head tilted back, eyes closed, mouth open but mute,

ready to receive the mark of divine beauty,
    the metic's claritas, wherein might be glimpsed

through the glaucomatous tears of gonorrhea
    one's shimmering, orthopedic image.

This getting back what you didn't give is time
    in the same way one still says 'play' and 'game'

but with unanticipated meanings from without,
    or you reach for your Beretta and pull a 1911 out

from under your shirtwaist, first as tragedy,
    second as joke in your town. Breaking into

the clear black night, the clear white moon of his head
    emerges capless from a veil of smoke that like a hood

donates the mentor's perilous umbra to his sage antlers,
    paged to quest for his pay, his paisano, whom he finds

in the 213 getting jacked in the midst of a dice game
    gone sour. He steps from his ride, approaching the scuffle,

and before his features even resolve, his gat
    explodes, he squeezes the trigger as he feels it unload,

and piece dripping spent caps, having thus busted them
    in their punk asses, he switches his mind back into freak mode.

Over the din of dropped bodies and bass, his voice comes alive.
    "Say my name," he intones, and the chorus reports:

"Killa Beez, man-maker, scourge of twink-ass bitches,
    hardest wigger with the itchiest trigger, says 'please'

"and 'thank you' while up to his shank in you."
    Resumes Killa Beez, addressing the boy he just saved:

"So if you want blouses, young squire, sit back and observe—
    I just left a gang of those over there on the curb."

And so Killa Beez and Project Patroclus
    return to the scene of the stranded demoiselles

and escort them to the Eastside Motel where,
    with a wink and a nod and in twin queens,

Project Patroclus and Killa Beez watch
    each other fuck these freak damsels. Now,

when the child of morning, brown-fingered
    dawn, appeared, the hero, Killa Beez, rose

and dressed himself, addressing himself
    to his ward *a cappella*, as did Artemis

to Callisto in leather, castigating the youth,
    ringless and Rolexless, for getting jacked shooting dice:

"Project Patroclus, why won't you put away
    this childish game, these *alea* of Palamedes?

"Have you learned nothing from his encounter
    with the odious hater? A liar by virtue bars no holds.

"Are you not better than some horny trick?
    Are you, like some weaker vessel, so easily moved?

"Or have you taken instead a page from
    Cappellanus, using jealousy to grease love?

"Alas! 'tis Sacred Jealousie, Love rais'd to an Extream.'
    You see, when grief at the death of my virtue

"revealed to me the force of my love for it,
    I consented to make peace with my brother

"and to out his bitch as a deceiver—her beauty
    a peruke, a hair mat that on divestment proves

"beauty inheres not in each skull, however neotenic.
    'Tis true of all women." "All women?" asks Project

Patroclus, "Are they all one?" "They are to me,"
    replies Killa Beez. "Pounded and surrounded

"or put out to pasture, their teats grown
    milk-long, their noon-bright halos set,

"hanging like misshapen, jeweless wreaths
    and with nurples purple as bed sores, they rub

"our faces in their fugly dugs to pinchbeck us,
    cruel, heartless creatures that take pleasure

"from our suffering. Should we then expect
    a woman to understand what passes between

"two men on the field of battle? 'Twould be
    unreasonable and unfair. To lift them up

"only worsens their fateful fall, which, however
    self-inflicted, is their sole leverage and last resort.

"A girl uncanted is fit only to pray
    and fine booty just war spoils.

"I'm reminded of the Athenian rascals and cutters
    who at the advice of the army disbander

"held their cunts and made demands.
    Remember how foul bitch Princess Peach

"to send us all on terminal shore leave
    up-sold Legal Aid as a glabrous idiot, as if

"we were some rustic Ruskins to be had
    or one-eyed senators waving ones at cloying Theory,

"in effect a bald but bearded Venus, her face
    reflected in her own pate, as if in patent leather,

"*patefacio* in the capital Forum, where is erected
    a temple to those pockmarked *castrati,*

"twin bullocks whose own reluctance to bar
    holds brought us here? So if all's fair,

"all that's fair's put our boots to dunes
    and got that fraunch dike-plugging Palamedes

"caught in his tent with his bunny fric-plaunted full
    of bones struck with eagle-crowned *Colonna Traiana.*"

Sick of the tongue lashing and wishing he'd have had
    the false choice to lose his life at the hands of those high

rollers than to have to live it held in the hands
    of this his so-called brother equally dad-less

but no more emancipated, Project Patroclus
    replies to Killa Beez beratement, saying,

"The way the wind blows, daddy Aggie
    will lose his head for sure. But you?

"You'll just end up undead on white Elba
    with ocean sunrise, relaxing while at your side

"a doe-eyed, dick-whipped *pharmakos* gently
    whispers, *'Te amat bellum non iam para,'*

"stoking your bucolic hankering for a piece
    everlasting, offshored minting of specious fiat

"lodged in the skull of a brown child on which some
    numismatist to come might misread your legend.

"I say this with a whore's pipes: I wish to be
    interpellated otherwise. I want not to be

"kept alive in your memory by your ritual fucking
    of *Herr* Hektor, corpse of a thousand-year Reich.

"No man is a hero to his valet-de-chambre, and this footnote's
    so far up your ass, it speaks in your same voice.

"In this do I side with the bold Lesbian who jeered you
    mourning your love—my accidental avenger, dangling

"on the end or your sword—that cur of envy
    who tore the eyes from your ideal and called me

"your 'bitch,' crusty batch of nature who
    you rode in covered wagon through passion gap.

"He is the smudge of shit in your mustache, orator,
    a bad debt not even the cunning unnamed can write off.

"He's the tell-all you were too proud to be
      and so gave up ignominy for an epic. But I remember.

"This devilishly sweet bread, amnesiac madeleine,
      ushers the letter I scratch out, the wrong one,

"the evil one, so that it still overtakes you
      in its remanance, which is nothing less

"than the remanence of the will in the fallen
      spirit. So in this one weak vessel,

"in this one bone locker, are we
      bound like imperial faggots.

"You are my incurable bone ache,
      and I, a shit medic. Spurred tibia and boned spirit.

"Your frontale resting on my temporale;
      your phalanges brushing my femur.

"And so I remember, but I remember badly.
      I can speak, but my teeth only mark

"off a sacred area, a garden even more
      precise and precious than the rest of the forest.

"And in chewed-over words, I bare witness
      to your passion, in which, with one blow,

"loose-tongued Thersites you defanged,
      that candid dandy, my uncanny Cunégonde,

"his fag end a star in the dark of hell's alley
      toward which into uncertainties I now steer alee."

Chorus

A generic experiment in whiteface and straight drag, which ventrilo-quizes manly speech, resisting the impulse to name its subject so as not to relapse into its unavoidable jingoism but instead to make it apparent in its poor performance. The masks slips a little, a poor fit in the first place. Self-mastery is betrayed in that space, which requires the illusion of such mastery so as to open up at all, since to expose the farce as such would not effect the stage machinery that seeks only its own repetition regardless of who's cast. So then, to perform it badly. Only in the total identification of actor and role, of essence and appearance, does their difference shine out.

Plato was critical of acting, finding in it a horrifying confusion of essences and appearances that he considered detrimental to public order. Ruled by passions, the audience cannot distinguish between the actor and their role, and if the audience can believe it, then what's the effective difference between the two? While the answer might seem ob-vious, Plato's concern reveals an anxiety about what is appropriate when it comes to being and appearing and what is the appropriate re-lation between an appearance and its essence. But the actor is not only a big fuck you to what's appropriate, they also disturb the possibility of policing that relation. It can't be accidental that Plato takes for his ex-ample an actor playing the role of a general. His anxiety concerning acting is really his anxiety concerning how to order people, specifically how to get people to be the things they supposedly already are. It's not enough to force people to be a certain way, Plato's all about guarantees, so he needs some guarantee, a transcendental faculty that can locate in reality the distinction between classes. And he says he's found that faculty in reason.

Plato thinks that by appealing to the essences of things, the transcen-dental faculty of reason can escape the democratic confusion of ap-pearances and demonstrate how types of people should be limited to their appropriate social classes. The problem for Plato is, if essence is supposed to be more fundamental than and determinate of appearance, then how come appearance can so easily flaunt essence? If no necessary relationship between essence and appearance obtains, then on what grounds can the faculty of reason make its distinctions? So Plato brings in another faculty, situated in the soul between reason and the passions. He calls it *thumos* (meaning at the same time "pride," "indignation," and "shame"), and its job is to separate essences and appearances, because clearly essences, despite their essentiality, can't help but cavort with those seductive and capricious appearances.

Thus actors and poets have to be banished instead of being reeducated, since there's really nothing to reeducate them on—they've already seen the essence of essences, and it ain't pretty. There's no place for poets and actors except outside of the walls of the polis, and what keeps them there is *thumos*, which is not an attribute of reason but is its own faculty and which can be understood as something akin to patriotism.

II.

And so, having crossed the bar, the spirit
    of Patroclus no longer authors any action

against his slaver, Achilles. No harmony issues
    from the grave—the lay rarely outlives the lyre,

wise tokens from Simmias to knavish Socrates
    as the latter abandoned his hierarchy of traits

and went paraparetically (or was it "peripatetically"?)
    on his way to get degaussed. What a burden it would be

to recall everything. Were it such, wouldn't we,
    fresh from the womb, lay down and not stir

until we starved or froze or had our brains
    dashed out by some weak-hearted midwife

so moved? Instead, a soul is mercifully reset
    by the indecipherable mark, the flipped bit,

that springs from the *fontenelle* of youth.
    Thus the trauma of birth is the only true *katharsis*.

It's what it means to be a monstrous abbreviation.
    Something else is like, "I got this."

So, in this way, it is our right
    to die in the port of Rashid

leaving no unturned stone, temporal banality
    being only the processing of bit rot,

the bony entropy function, but like,
    super-fucking-pixelated bones, no more

telling at close range. These bones go
    to rest beneath the fallen stone

that forms the blind alley of Iphigenia's cenotaph,
    here, at Brauron, where we are reunited

with Theory in the form of nubile fuzzy-
    wuzzies in berserker teddies,

a procession of ursine fursonas casting
    childish things ("Never till now esteemed

Toyes") into the sacred spring,
    dousing themselves in the blood of sacrificial

deer now roasting on the alter to Artemis,
    that stainless Shakespearean butcher,

and in stripping down do these anti-exports
    propitiate the beaver queen

who would pin the conditions of material life
    on the purity of young girls,

as seen in the legend of the humbling of Patras,
    whose satrap Petraeus was forced to suck

napalm from the tip of a cluster bomb strapped
    on to Artemis' doe-skin harness.

The maternity wear of new mothers
    is burnt to the goddess, though the shrouds

of matricided parturients go to Iphigenia,
    and from their mingled smoke, the spirit

of everything that has lived and died
    before now advances like the war-machine

that James Hetfield could only uncritically
    figure as Cthulhu, hunter of the shadows.

Instead, the paracusia that deathly growls
    from the earbuds of the private's GNTX ACH

and the technician's BAE Systems ACH—
    pathos of knowledge that spurs service—

does not lead to the sleep of reason. The sleep
    of reason is a means to its total deployment.

Everything finds its way back to the center
    in one form or another. Rabble succored

with casualty. Rubble secured with flag pin.
    We are segued to the gift shop by armed crooners

whose intestines, like yellow ribbons,
    adorn the trembling lapels of eulogists

who dedicate their queefing deixes, and who,
    from their pricey mount on a heap of human offal,

beg us turn our eyes skyward, where might be
    glimpsed falling the soul of an ostracized Platonist

party barged and fleeced by a gang
    of fanatical sacristans cracking hostile lambs

on their chasm, chunking flutes in the fireplace,
    and scratching a prehistoric pornography

by the light of the archive on fire,
    sacked and halved like our Alexandrine mather.

The city remains if only in the needlework MATRIX
    of generalized exchange of mothers, daughters, sisters

between the killers of fathers, husbands,
    brothers, sons similarly spear-won

by leaf-broad head, bronze butt-spike,
    and ash, another caved-in drag queen

carved out in Achilles' penetrating light, stet
    that triumphal column of black light dropping

from the oculus to scan the marble of the dome's floor,
    where one—Briseis, Iphigenia, Iphys, Hypatia—

was left, waiting to disappear into
    the unintelligible speech of the smoking men,

cheek cool on faux marble countertop
    and veiled in her own inverted skirts.

Back at camp, the uplink sends photos of home
    along with the drone's green feed—our eyes,

like hardpoints on a Reaper's wing—
    and as in a headshot, we are taken in one gesture,

the flirty curl of a finger, not to come
    to leave but to become a pure

voluptuousness that is for us
    indistinguishable from humiliation,

to be betrayed by our own corpuses,
    hardon in theater, soft symposium

in the brig. I've given my vigilance over
    to wretchedness, as have you.

Upon the double string of our eyes is marched
    the orthopedic image of a pornstar

getting our labor power fucked out of her.
    She sees to him to seem to be seen by him,

while we only see his cum turn to mucus,
    his *munus* turn to go. He is resorbed

into the individual by soul-voluptuousness,
    by the child-king's jubilant assumption of the throne.

Having up to now been ass-fed the body
    of Christ, I'm relieved to choke on D and not B,

on an orange agent and not agent orange, eyes
    tearing up from the ash pouring down my cock holster.

I know on this next sortie I'll have to perform
    Tiny Elvis on a muter dashboard for my fellow soldiers.

For now, I dry fire into a clearing
    barrel while browsing PRISM,

clean up with the regimental groundsheet,
    and lie about where I put it.

This is precisely how the spirit of Patroclus
        and all the dead, Greek and Trojan, atone

for the letter copied out in monkish hand
        by a hunky man cassocked in dim *dimanche*,

his sad cock firmly canted at an
        encountered concubine he's just transcribed

and underscored in itchily triggered ditz and dahs,
        spelling out the ensuing eulogy in the spirit's spit,

which brings to mind the bone
        on which it comes to choke.

Addressing battle-wyfies rounded up
        and pious female soldiers laid

white as ash amid funereal cypresses,
        it says, "No day shall erase you

"from the memory of time." As if
        it's time that remembers what time's left.

It nods in the immediate seizure of decision, form
        wrested from the contented practice of the multitude

going about their hours, days, months, years—
        an eon marking time in furrows and pruned fig leaves.

Chorus

In Aristophanes' play *Peace*, in which the gods abandon Olympus to its new tenant, War, the character of Theory is a prostitute the protagonist Trygaeus tries to pimp to the Senate. Aristophanes plays on the sense of theory as "contemplation," turning it into something conspicuous, something all too visible, which the eye devours and which devours the eye.

The Republic begins with Socrates returning from "theorizing," that is, watching the religious spectacles (*theoria*), in Piraeus. As the dialogue progresses, the *theoria* of the festival is supplanted by the *theoria* of philosophic speculation. Plato argues that philosophers are similar to the lovers of sights and sounds who follow the festivals of Dionysus (like goofy deadheads) from town to town to witness the spectacles, except that philosophers are "lovers of the sight of truth." But the festivals of Dionysus are lewd affairs, which suggests that truth is maybe something not a little raunchy and that looking at truth is perverse.

The traditional characterization of the pure contemplation of Platonic forms as something noble is perhaps misguided to the extent that it does not take into account the perversity of the spectator of truth, who comes off not unlike like Pentheus in Euripides *Bacchae*, sneaking off to spy on the bacchantes (including his mother and aunt) in the throes of their erotic frenzy. Even if truth were pure, the love of truth would still be pathological.

That explains (though in no way excuses) the author's interest in the rhetoric of Dylan Klebold in general and, in the case of the present work, that of Elliot Rodger (whose fatally laughable manifesto, "My Twisted World," appears heavily redacted as Telemachus' monologue). What he finds in this rhetoric is a deep insecurity about Rodger's own status as a man. The truth discovered in Rodger's words is not literal, that is, it does not mean what it says, but it can't say what it means without telling us nothing. The truth of his histrionics is his desire to be a beautiful blond white girl, but for the poem (or him, for that matter) to come right out and say it would not give us (or him) the truth of that desire, only its object. And not because truth is some ineffable ethere-ality or that it is 'just too big' to be described by our measly little words. Truth can never be put into words because words only lie, but it is be-cause words only lie that truth appears negatively as a possibility.

So the best allegory for truth is still that of Plato's cave, though no one, not even Plato, could actually read it. The emphasis is usually put on the blinding brightness of the sun and the (equally) blinding darkness of the cave, but truth is not the sun (nor, conversely, the darkness of the cave and paleness of the fire), instead, truth is the time it takes to adjust from one to the other. Walking out into the light or back into the cave, there is a period of time in which you have to let your eyes adjust. Truth is what doesn't let you transition between inside and outside without exacting a little payment in the form of your inability to witness.

III.

As the pliant wax is stamped
    with new designs and is no longer

what once it was, but changes
    form, and still is pliant wax, so too

is the spirit of Patroclus evermore the same
    though passing to ever-changing bodies.

Quartered, a reinstated Patroclus reclines
    in the bed of a deported patriarch. One hand

hangs over the edge, twirling a lock of hair
    on the head of the daughter sleeping there;

the other unbuttons the top of his shirt,
    revealing the cleft of his enormous breasts.

He pulls one out and gives his nipple
    a pinch, milking his pink tit with his palm.

Out the window, the dark of the surrounding
    suburb is punctured by pools of streetlamp light;

the cool night air is punctuated with gunfire
    and the erratic crinkle of personal property

under tread. Several drunk soldiers are busy
    trying to flush a naked girl from some bushes.

Through the bedroom door, Patroclus sees a handful
    of generals pass. One of them stops and sticks his head

in the room. "Son," he says, "have you seen a demonic
    "courtesan, 'bout yay high, goes by the name 'Theory'?"

Patroclus pops his right tit out of his mouth
    and, rising, steps over the young girl, making

his way to the open window, and planting
    one ass cheek on its clean sill, puts an unlit

cigarette to his lips. "Can't say," he replies.
    "Sure you can. She ain't hard to miss.

"For one, she's not much for talking,
    more a maid gunning for action, this one,

"usually flipping a coin in one hand, the other
    up to her elbow in her breadwinner

"frantically snatching cash-cube-like as much
    paperless chattel as she can war-rape whiter."

Patroclus shrugs and lights his cigarette.
    The generals (they'd all come into the bedroom

at this point) resume their search—all but General
    Telemachus, prince to a bloody Ibiza unto himself.

The boy is pharm-fresh—backlit but not without
    razor burn. His pout, a self-seriousness captured

in prepubescent chunk. His eyes have the hyper-
    vigilant squinch of a drone pilot. He speaks:

"The video showed him stick his penis
    inside a girl's vagina. I had never seen

"what beautiful girls looked like naked,
    and the fair sight filled me with strong

"and overwhelming emotions. The power
    that beautiful women have is unbelievable.

"You see, I am an intellectual who is
    destined for greatness. For instance,

"I would never perform a low-class service job.
    Both my friends James and Philip seem to be

"the weak, accepting type; whereas I am the fighter.
    My destiny was to fight against the unfairness of the world.

"Yet, while I was at father's house, I wasn't able
    to do my five-hour-long events to collect rare

"armor pieces for my <SELF>. You see, I had
    become very powerful, and I was in one of the best

"guilds. With this guild, I participated in lots of raid
    events to collect better gear and armor for my <SELF>.

"Being rich, I thought, will definitely make me
    attractive enough to have a beautiful girlfriend.

"My father never made any effort
    to prepare me for facing such a cruel world.

"He never taught me how to attract girls.
    What a weak man. I eventually grew

"to hate him after I heard him having
    sex with my sister: I arrived at the house

"one day, my mother being at work, and heard
    the sounds of Odysseus plunging his penis

"into my sister's vagina through her closed door,
    along with my sister's moans. I stood there

"and listened to it all. I was so enraged that
    I almost splashed him with my orange juice.

"And so my starvation began. It was,
    as the phrase that I had coined goes,

"'the comfort before the storm.' Other boys
    were allowed to experience the pleasures of sex,

"all because girls didn't want me.
    I seriously started to consider working towards

"writing an epic story. I was always creating
    stories in my mind to fuel my fantasies.

"Usually those stories depicted someone
    like myself rising to power after a life

"of being treated unfairly. I delved more into learning
    as much as I could from books at Barnes & Noble.

"I expanded on the political and philosophical
    ideals I concocted when I was seventeen,

"and I soon became even more radical
    about them than I ever was before.

"To sum it all up for you, here's the thesis
    I developed: Women are sexually attracted to

"the wrong type of man. This is a major flaw
    in the very foundation of humanity."

With this Telemachus lays on his back
    and pulls his knees up to his chest.

The hem of his tunic rides up on his stomach
    and his penis flops toward his face like a weather-

cock blown south, his tightening scrotum
    unveiling the seam that runs along

his frottage-depilated taint, the seam where
    he'd been stuffed and darned on his first day.

"It's as if it's this seam," thinks Patroclus, "that he wants
    me to undo with Achilles' sovereign ray."

"Did it work?" Telemachus asks.
    "Am I yet a beautiful blond woman?"

"No," replies Patroclus. "You are just, like,
    a mind engaged with new and temporary things,

"an indelible smudge banal in its singularity,
    a folk tradition mistaken for city management."

And so at this, Telemachus shits
    out the severed dicks of a hundred suitors,

thudding one on top of the other under
    the purple flower of his bodiless cunt.

"My misogyny is ironic," he continues, "because
    I don't have the physical, political, or emotional

"power to hurt women. They have the power
    to hurt me, and have, and continue to do so.

"My sexual conquests are limited, and
    I've always been a gentleman to them,

"ever grateful and loving, but I have not
    yet been born. My body hasn't arrived

"hooked, like lamb, in its crate, so what
    I look out of now, my current insertion point,

"is a kind of limbo, a ventilator
    for my vegetal spirit, while I wait for that which

"aligns itself with what the girls
    at Plato's Closet call the 'commodity form.'

"The females of the human species are
    incapable of realizing the value in me.

"Throated and throttled, they threaten me
    with what I can never have: a crammed lumen

"cock-occupied and, as always, unwarranted,
    though never warrantless; a rosy and civic

"cockcrow glorious and holy." Bored, Patroclus turns away
    and leaning out the window dictates

in a degraded dialect and in cloven-cadenced
    homophony to birds that transcribed each letter

partitioned by equal signs in diffident flight
    a circadian recounting of his childhood in Wonder City.

"I deny it. Thick were sawn thatcher sores,
    wards in the hay, ends of knots. This tarred

"her lack of twin-tease, easy-bake ovens and days in sin.
    Fools rushed in and said in the wind a sigh—

"an AM wave in gob-eyed ether. Ask,
    'How tough am I that furs to maim him well?'

"The black adolescent egged a Range Rover,
    but I'd upped your fore-undoer, and 'twas over-rusted.

"I'd Edened Eve in giftware dimed as pity,
    but dead-end Eve had a letch who took her higher.

"Yet how in doubt? How's a Yahweh dead—
    formed with a putsch or nigh a fiesta?

"I was wino-toilet tagged; I was sorrow who sinned
    and who stood even as he stung a star addled

"as a naked doe, and sung lasses tore eyes to all.
    Why'd you go love, son, a midge? It collected a deer

"sown in a piece of barbwire the black doges leafed.
    A slag underdone was capped.

"'Away, my gun,' lowed a dove. Deb
    budded to fly the queefer *en masse* to us

"when the drawers turned wan and gay
    like my Nora within Janet's sore D&D.

"Haints of the father that matched his shun
    came e'en to thick rancor, tended to seduce law.

"I owned the bane, the kith in night court,
    the trawlers that hone Keystone Light.

"Keystone spurned in sip, and a cyst twirled
    to see as hag a lady noble and then rested assured

"its bride was a madrigal offal. Dirty preacher in Tupelo
    went and fell all around the peahen, hollering 'Fie! Rise!'

"Autumn's half-turd, a few newer hollerers
    at room paid to grate pelt. I pissed on a lawn, today.

"My threat to dub blacks just wasn't gazed but a tatty gig
    at history. Then Memphis dads cooed a fit in wooden garret.

"Aggies whizzed into night. The easy treasure been grabbed,
    but it was still cool to tease that blonde fissure.

"Me and you were two clover hawks, jugs he used to be
    mawing over, or semen he gets enough on our pie plate.

"Lye. Quim. A kiss. Her honor lips weren't easy on the tip.
    Peons of the shyest aid tipped who I doubt they're owed it.

"Turrell lugs lied in a gash-ark or in Josie's tug,
    a heist-pig that was in need of the pool we bang in.

"A plover, this dove ended us alone.
    Thus she dowsed in the ray of terse, thistly flora.

"E'en his knots dumped, teased hard.
    E'en Cains fooled and oft aided pool-sin.

"A ray in woe hit her distal states.
    They played hunk's thighs, eased in,

"and parsed three buff though wooly if leave-in,
    dirt-rapping, stanchion-blued fine horses.

"The attack of merkins pried a sinner, socked that hoe,
    and jammed blues on the wah-wah, churl-hawked guitar.

"Didn't even inch up that torn aid—hosed it down.
    I ain't do woo. It was under a deer, so gone.

"I was pay-per-gay Jan, a diet-ache in a bay as in a war.
    She'd up a mom and a crow I'd wear out with lye

"and sewn-up fur. Tombs hyper-saw this
    team boa. Doug owned too the Opry in you.

"War, a lens; the aught, a gray fuzz.
    All about us, her daybed may have ended.

"She cooed Morman high chirrs in a teen-tag
    and inched her Rimbaud leech in his fain chosen.

"A rainbow muscled in, thumbed who in the lot
    lacked more chaos tenets than tobacco czars.

"The forced churn in the Arkabutla showed
    now a fur vee, and innocent sin wished a doe gassed

"on the beige, thick rave that defied all that's hers,
    whether be hauling issues or hawk-inch rims.

"The diazepam care-free wan must have walked
    in hatchery hymns, wet off ichor-red sleep.

"The sly cads lied to the camera. An aunty erred like
    a pause in a dynamo, like a mossed, sea-alkaline sliver

"as I would dare some slights and minty reflection.
    Coulda hemmed limb-fuss. Ain't life cruel?

"It like it hung onto Lee. In a sense, the lie coulda been
    took, but compliant the foe lay dead nigh the fifth roan.

"An impasse dove rough. A lame lock fizzled.
    Got par to get it on. Lager evolved when hurled

"outta tin pools, and law guns blasted oily wads.
    The law grew porn to lock up lugs. Twelve-sided

"die lagged, and sheep swilled spoons for a free stir.
    In a tree, I was locked to wool, fleeing Jason's tail.

"On all fours, Elsie lumped nookie to cease
    the maw in me currently due to her perp-hell

"and meth, just a lych-gate of Huguenot meringues.
    Heady knot-ins annulled your brogue.

"Joining Alise, I was bawdy, eased pee
    in tennis hay, and undid a simulant.

"Eased in and joined Alise to a white boy,
    a coward tinny Yasmine aught to have pit too.

"As phys-ed gym wood e'en eyed me,
    ut Seius edere sapo, zippers dared young'uns.

"Homie tethered sod to adjust the motto,
    showed you're your legal chain.

"An eddied hymn hainted steady with no pause.
    Easy dawn in the USA, her din-din no jizz.

"Heard me say, 'Addend voices and gun the null-set
    thanks to no soupy fur in May.' Today

"the gun's dry, finds a daffy hush for Friday to stray.
    Saw him wore anadems gone at Turin; saw him run,

"whisked to hell while a boa was dad's bouquet.
    Tried to pee on an ichthus-tatted teat, through which

"a willow's eyes peeked. A ribbon, a pill, a limb allayed my cuss-head,
    although a disused *soleil* wouldn't loan dad a key.

"He lied eloped, de-trou'd, damned in hymn's law,
    low sin—her knee, why it assayed, churned so.

"Hauled the lawn that day. A mean town of caustic pews,
    cannons, hangings, whence limbs thrown to decedents,

"and rowdy pay-per-view pee-cage in dun towel,
    were each day a din e'en prayer-kisses couldn't negate.

"Indeed, I toyed Kim to be no tepid earner. How
    'no way' meant not to hose her with his woody.

"Con menu of bitter *bona fides* in mass in woulda-been-
    sweetest war couldn't open me pecans I have. Fecal dawn.

"Somebody was asphyxiating Donna Tucker. Their noose
    taught cinch-zip from Chickasaw Gardens

"toward a once-trying finalism. In a dress knitted
    from atomic weed, needs whirred under my kilt.

"He pooled dentists, bought Hummers, leaped woodies,
    but he was just another dad-bout; he was trained on coon whine.

"Faith cure-alls got a sister died fighting us.
    Pitied bag of nachos out-twined faith.

"Rare was when Becky said 'Woowee, boy!' Tom went,
    and a boy peed. I had driven Wayne to war.

"Lambs dared stark fays Yahweh's mild airs of disaster.
    Nice, toothy god of the briny key cutter, Thanatos,

"seduced hot pay in spite of my démodé phooey-
    teased stomach spinning Jews in deluded crown.

"Thick daughter wowed swarded hymns
    in a thanks a chump could pun.

"Denny starred a good anonym for Sylvie,
    who kept saying, 'Woowee!'

"Chesty demos keyed hosiery with their pig meow,
    queefed true, and raided the true team who brawled.

"A crow rode up on horsey poo. It was faith
    cured Annie's mouthy whistle day-laid in sin.

"Dad abetted fear's effort to hide my lugged doubt.
    Twin dose of amatol maimed Nora's data,

"some eye data thitherly ersatz. No groin we weaned,
    a crawdad was up on the edge, and I could see them

"trailing alongside to pose the dead in mud,
    dead they couldn't animate as downtrodden.

"The town's hawk tail bided wars innocuously. Eden mud
    tugged her dead eye a rude inch, and weaned a doughy elder,

"tying my marauding to pine hush odors beyond sin.
    I ain't God. I was too togged." And with that, Patroclus dies,

again, only to come to on blanc Alba, under a wretched
    sun, solstitial and pendulous, strolling alongside

immortal, unkillable, irrepressible Achilles
    who, without waiting to be asked, begins,

"We assumed there would be consolation enough."
    Shrugging, he gestures to the landscape and to the few

pale youths who languish in grass-stained tennis whites,
    and continues, "Having chosen in depthless acreage

"a destiny foreshadowed only by lately retracted teats.
    All signs pointed to yesterday, but we declined,

"or rather demurred. What future is the negation of all
    known futures? There is a power in the tautology

"of such total rebellion, the strategy-less tactics
    of a stiff-armed youth. A port in any storm, we thought.

"My friend, the weather has improved, is finally
    indifferent, and yet I've no tackle for calm, no

"stomach for still waters. I mean, look, all
    my metaphors are maritime. When's the last time

"you traveled by boat? I've certainly never been
    'out at sea.' A Somali pirate might find my figures,

"however inapplicable, at least legible.
    But those in the vicinity, to whom I am

"bound simply by the limitations of time, space,
    and income, would they give these anachronisms

"the benefit of the doubt? I'm all thumbs,
    and wooden thumbs at that. Each caress

"leaves a trail of splinters; each connection,
    a grating twang of modem jargon, unwelcome

"and uncomfortable, like Bradley tracks on seashells.
    A language starred by necessity, a patois,

"the wording of which worsens into a version of that
    against what it was first uttered. A declaration of love

"that comes out as a strangled 'My word!' whipping
    across the face of a twin to my primordial snubber,

"the thread of whose lie loops back to a child's word
    spoken in the lethal passion of innocence,

"the meaning of which, though clear to me now,
    seems to have been half spoken in merciful deferral,

"that is until this very moment when, with the pink
    smart of this rebuff, its full significance is realized

"even in its final exit left. A tongued barrel categorical in
    the vagueness of its recall, in the belatedness of its recoil.

"That moment, impossible as it is, is thus forever
    immediate to the guillotine of its decision.

"It's arrival, or rather, mine, is hindered by such dumb matter
    that its penetration becomes an irresistible course.

"Until then, I remain, suspended in the inconsummate
interval of retarded fondles, simply Achilles."

Chorus

Looking is always looking *from* somewhere; it's not determined by the object of its vision. Plato understands this implicitly, and *thumos,* as patriotism or, as we argue, police, is first introduced in a little vignette about a looky-loo and some rotting corpses. Leontius, coming to Athens along the long wall from the port city of Piraeus sees the bodies of a bunch of executed criminals lying outside the wall. Despite his initial disgust at the sight, his desire to see gets the better of him, such that he throws his eyes open in the direction of the corpses, and says, "Look, ye wretches, take your fill of the fair sight!"

The moral of the story for Plato isn't, why are people so perverted, ew? Instead, he immediately considers the subjective technologies for withdrawing value from the passion to look and subordinating them under its opposite, reason. The assumption he makes is that the baseness of such desires requires that it be disciplined out of the individual and, extrapolating from the allegory of Leontius, disciplined out of the state as well. But, according to Plato's own view of things, what is base should be powerless and should simply decompose. What value does reason have if it is powerless against the desire to stare at dead bodies? As something that tills the hard soil of essentiality and necessity, shouldn't its perfection be assured? Yet what obtains in actuality is not reason but base passion; what is base does not decay but proliferates instead.

It's this powerlessness of reason that gives philosophy its main task, which is to make up shit that makes up for the fact that what should be yet isn't. In Plato, this made-up shit is precisely *thumos*, which in the soul marshals the passions to generate in a person a strong desire for reason. In the state, *thumos* is just the police. The police make sure that everyone does what they're told and tells them. Thus, it would seem that Plato affirms that which he sets out to deny in the first part of *the Republic:* the definition of justice given by Thrasymachus, that justice "is nothing else than the interest of the stronger."

The whole history of philosophy is just a succession of systems that establish what is necessary as such and then go on to explain why that which is necessary does not obtain in actuality. The latter is often explained by reference to the devil or original sin or, in Plato's case, mimesis or, more generally, human fallibility, which in our time takes the form of human fallibility in relation to the efficiency of market forces, specifically that of state intervention in markets. The global market is a fantastical ideal whose inherent perfection is paradoxically perturbed by the intervention of regulatory apparatuses. Of course, it is precisely state intervention that sustains the market—it's just that we call it Operation Enduring Freedom or Operation Neptune's Spear. The point is, because we mistakenly believe that this is the best of all possible worlds, the inexistent necessity of such ideals (freedom, the market, human dignity) makes the perfect alibi for the global security apparatus against the litany of impediments to its arrival: thugs, feminists, terrorists, immigrants, the disabled, welfare queens, drug addicts—the list is structurally interminable. The efficacy of this alibi is that its confirmation is infinitely postponable. In place of necessity's appearance is the continual purification of the place of its appearance. In what form does the "pride" and "shame" of *thumos* appear in our time except that of patriotism, literally "brotherhood"?

IV.

On Alba in black night, the sweet recess of eve,
    and out from under the neighborhood watch,

a lacustrine and centurial magnolia hid two lovers
    feathered wet on the rail of a black bough.

Rosie's finger crooks, her knuckles blooded by bark,
    bark of the same thick branch she straddles

flabbily snaking canopied mud, her vertebrae locked
    tongue-and-groove in the knurred and furrowed trunk.

Backed into Rosie, heel hiked in the crotch of two branches,
    Dawn's globes grip the bough's coarse bark,

her hair anointed in a blossom's creamy citrus,
    leaves speaking continuously in sibilants together.

Gusted by wind, the bootjack limb tugs her wider,
    the meat of Rosie's hand mats down Dawn's tuft,

thumbnail raking ginger whorls and
    snapping the rubbery knurl tendinous

in the fork of fusiform furrows,
    the sound of teeth nipping in concavity,

ripping the wax leaves' soft crack, bump, and clack,
    index and nameless pinning sepals and corolla

like monarch wings to the crooks of Aurora's crura,
    like an ace knucklebone rattling around the most

beautiful Artemisian calix at the Symposium, when
 horizonal, the astrologer's cock-crown Lucifer

("a knave that moves as light as leaves by winde"),
 from the cab of his snowy Bronco emblazoned

New Day Security Inc. whips his out his Maglite
 and on the magnolia lets fall from it his Phoeban spear.

But the tree's dense, dendritic limbs and waxen,
 shield-like leaves deflect the grave blades of light

and hide the culpable loveres so depe in-with its hollow.
 And when the beam parts, the bristled couple duck out,

disturbing the scaly canopy of their hideaway hive.
 Toward the sound the beam whirls, illumining only

the lustrous wings of ducks bedding down
 near one the development's many ponds.

Shot so from the bolt, Dawn collapses in a bed
 of pine-straw near a row of Grecian laurel.

Rosie kneels over her. "Muscle up, babe.
 Not quite out of the woods."

At that, Dawn reaches out with both hands
 and cupping Rosie's chin fixes to her own

the other's eyes in whose abysses swarm
 a plenitude of thoughts half formed. She says,

"Why niltow over me hove, as longe as whanne
 Almena lay by Jove? And for the love

"of God that us bath wrought, lat in your brayn
        non other fantasye so crepe, that it cause me to dye."

And upon this slumber party bearded Venus smiled,
        donating her Phi Theta Kappa pin to aid them.

And night passed, and Rosie, glancing the pin in its straw
        bed and glancing in it the light of nearing dawn, said

"Hail, gladdening light," their first in this their first bed
        from which they now must part as two lips part to cuss.

Chorus

So brotherhood requires an inexistent ideal, in this case a shared potency, and a swath of obstacles or threats to that ideal, which since we're talking about a group of men, are generally women. But potency is often correlated with an ideal of feminine beauty, which when lacking hinders that potency. So the inexistent ideal which guides the policing activity of a big group of men is ideal feminine beauty. This is why Helen of Troy is such an important figure. Helen is the symbol for the coupling in male fantasy of eroticism and animosity, the gesture that both caresses and throttles, that which is fair in both love and war.

In the figure of Helen, we can see a fundamental ambivalence in male-dominated society toward the female body. It is at once the vessel of the appearance of ideal feminine beauty and also the damned thing that gets in the way of that appearance and so must be disciplined. Women are always aging or gaining weight or cutting off their hair or wearing men's clothes or not wearing make up. The nerve! Can't they see they're not getting us hard? Don't they care?

Ancient Greece was all about disciplining its women, and it had all these subtle citizenship categories that allowed them more control over some bodies than others. According to Demosthenes: "We have *hetairai* for pleasure, *pallakai* for the body's daily needs and *gynaekes* for the bearing of legitimate children and for the guardianship of our houses." Of these three, only the *gynaekes*, wives and mothers, are those who are, in a sense, citizens. They have some rights, however curtailed relative to free men, yet they are not sex slaves (*pallakai*) or courtesans (*hetairai*).

Hetairai, who were *metics* (something akin to 'resident alien'), were the only women allowed to attend and participate in symposia (though, let us not forget the flute girl, the *phaule auletris*, in Plato's *Symposium*, who cannot participate). They managed money, paid taxes, were educated, and while not citizens were also not slaves. The flute girls of the *Symposium*, however, were *pornoi*, prostitutes, sex slaves to be precise. It is obvious what Socrates thought of the flute, choosing to bed down for good with the lyre, whose harmonic unity of melody and accompaniment was visible in the lengths and thicknesses of the strings, while the monody of the flute was a surreptitious mess of democratic combinatorics, a waste of breath.

The port of Athens, Piraeus, is the entry point for the *hetairai* and *pornoi*. It is the capital city's porous appendage. If Athens is the mind, Piraeus is its filthy body, its mouth, and its anus—the border that constructs (and polices) outside and inside, the tools of its survival and the risk of its exposure, bringing in slaves that Athens abhorred but on whom it so desperately depended. Piraeus touches what is other and thus risks being taken up in that otherness. Jacques Rancière writes that, "the whole political project of Platonism can be conceived as an anti-maritime polemic. The *Gorgias* insists on this: Athens has a disease that comes from its port, from the predominance of maritime enterprise governed entirely by profit and enterprise. The great beast of the populace, the democratic assembly of the imperialist city, can be represented as a trireme of drunken sailors. In order to save politics it must be pulled aground among the shepherds."

For Rancière, Plato's cave is a kind of anti-sea. Then what kind of anti-thing is his closet? The closet where the author as a child lay listening to the rush of water in the pipes toward shower heads, shooting out in thin jets onto the bodies of his family—water pulled from the filthy Mississippi with its barges and gambling boats? That's quite an intimate detail. If the cave is an anti-sea, then the closet is an anti-proscenium, like the wall behind which those who are neither captors nor prisoners carry shapes before the fire to cast shadows for those held hostage there.

V.

In the republic, buried in an outlandish slough,
    what is common gets passed around, a chafing

harness too big for us to buckle.
    It is this 'I' that needs exchanging, needs

to see its value totaled from
    the far side of transaction. Passed

around like cake, the feeling soon stales,
    and one goes out looking to rekindle

another, even littler easy-bake oven,
    hoping once and for all to get ours ate.

To be and to be on the clock
    are the two ticks of time's relentless bob.

In the republic, buried in an outlandish slough,
    an image of dawn-fucker Cephalus enjoying

my labor in the form of a flute girl working
    his column with the silence of her tool-entrusted

mouth. A cry. A column of sound from the throat
    passing undisturbed over teeth, tongue, and lips

(and since it's allegory and not fantasy,
    Cephalus here does not stand in for me).

It's this flute girl blowing bone who realizes
    my value, the value of my work, which is just

too much. Moreover, in this tainted looking glass,
    as a headless *mise-en-abyme*, I am fully employed

in my occupation. The cake-like division
    that is the truth of work is short circuited

in my different-born twin who writhing in
    a zero uncoiling like throttled hose consumes

without consummation, exhausting every
    pud that plugs her, and so, the hole she is

remains, teems with illegal mastery, autocratic
    fact, and every broken link of C-M-C that keeps

this legion from a regicidal infinite
    regression of recognized dependencies.

Opposite the image of the paid-to-play *auletris*,
    whose causal chain leashes her name to a service top,

the hole is the absence of lineage, of blood,
    being the war that being is, such that

simply existing is an affront, thrown itself
    headlong into disaster by no will of its own,

by no will at all, motorized by the duality
    it straddles: *für andere* and *für sich*.

The hole is full of starved thralls, legs broken
    in the fall, followed by starved dogs pitched in after,

mothers and daughters forced to swap spit
    off the rods of militiamen, dying of detached

cervices, lacerated uteri, bleeding out amid
    the incomprehensible speech of soldiers,

all able-bodied men and boys forced to kneel
    in a pool of crude set ablaze, men suffocating

under the bodies of men suffocating under
    the bodies of men castrated by dogs, corpses

bulldozed on top, their fence-blackened flesh
    dappled pink with burst blisters, as shit-

smeared cocks of quartered soldiers
    convulse in the throats of what's left.

The hole swarms with blood, cum, LFTB,
    and silicon, napalm, champagne, heroin, milk,

shit, sweat, oil and grease, sludge and slag,
    corn and soy and pink hormonal jism,

pork sausage, bacon, smoked salmon, sushi,
    filet mignon, roast chicken, roast potatoes, exactly

one severed finger along with its promise ring,
    and a cornfield's worth of boot-pulped putrefaction.

As an unengendered self-crapper,
    the hole does this under no name, countless

operator counting down. It's what doesn't
    stop your comrade from turning you in.

It's what doesn't keep your cake from molding.
    It's a cunning No-Man sodomizes you with

another's scepter, plants evidence, forges notes, is
    a POW of its own pud in Gitmo (as in "git mo' pussy")

on the long, strange trip back to the homeland.
    It unravels navels, spills guts, circumcises brides

and dons their stitched hoods as *larvatus prodeo*,
    and so disguised discloses the sheer probability

of its rudeness, and finding the officers with their pale
    fingers tangled in its wife's hair, joyfully takes her place.

And suppose once more, that he is reluctantly
    dragged. And suppose once more, that he is

reluctantly dragged up a steep and rugged ascent,
    out of the cave, the mine, the pit, out of

the spider hole, foxhole, trench, out from the
    rubble, out from under the fuselage, out of the crater,

the cloud of pulverized cement, out of the man
    cave, the kitchen, out from under his mother's skirts,

out of the memorial, the museum, out of his shirt, out of
    his winnings, his birthright, her mouth, out of her panties,

her fatigues. And now suppose that she is
    reluctantly dragged, Iphys, from her tent

by her CO for modified duty. The scene: DFAC.
    She cleans as General Patroclus leans back in a chair,

fingertips pinched in the top of his pockets,
    watching her tits sway in her green tank.

His hand moves to his thickness.
    The sibilant order to strip slips from his lips

like a snake's tongue, and in quick step
    he's up, and from back of his waistband, his 1911,

cocked, pressed to temple so's not to
    obscure the face, its expression, eyes

searching and ceasing to search as
    the barrel presses—only cool metal links

them, no force, no feigned ardor or
    token solicitation, revealing just the fact

of her ill fit, belonging only in the sense
    of chattel, belt buckle clinking on slab,

tipping her back onto table, his body
    heavy, shoulder pinning her throat,

sound from his chest felt more than heard.
    But just as the tip slips in, the goddess

ISIS, watching from her mount,
    with a word zips Iphys's slit.

The general pulls back, pinching his nipped tip,
    blood forces its way between his pinched fingers.

Her hairy labia balloon out into balls (her slit
    now only a seam) clit inflating, unfurling until

the purple, heart-shaped tip of her taut cock head,
    gleaming, mindlessly dribbles its sparkling juice.

The general crab walks back from the sight,
    his blood-drained snake flagging. Iphys

takes his pistol from the floor. —Turn over.
    —What? She pops him with the pistol's grip.

—Turn over. And straddling his thighs, she paints
    his asshole with precum, and as he looks back

with pleading eyes, she whips out her iPhone
    and snaps a pic of his wormed bud transfixed

on the anonymous rod jutting from a fresh
    set of thick pubes, which she then presses

to the dimpled cleft of his buttocks, eliciting
    a sissified bleat. In an act of treason,

the general's purpling sphincter involuntarily
    milks the root of her shaft, the pain

from its bracing contractions forces him
    actively to press down to relax his anus,

thus facilitating his own buggering,
    forced choice, and one thus at bottom desired.

Feeling this, Iphys donkey punches the general,
    retrieving the constriction and releasing her payload

deep into enemy territory. In the pic, his face
    is a tragedian's mask soon to be plastered

stateside on all the front pages, which will have him
    sucking on his own standard issue mercifully

smuggled into his cell by his old army buddies
　　in the days leading up to his court marshal.

But on this night, he whimpers *a cappella,*
　　as Iphys marvels at her manning and laments it,

thinking of what her sweet Ianthe,
　　who kept in her heart the image of a lover

Iphys no longer resembles, will think.
　　But on this very same night, in the stillness

of the homeland, the goddess ISIS
　　appears to Ianthe with the following annunciation:

"Ianthe, my ultraviolet, 'tis *Love,* and not
　　a thrice dipt Dart, that can Make you *Martyr* or

"her *Man.* Hers is the *Dart* must make the *Death*
　　Whose stroake shall taste thy hallow'd *breath*

"and you a milky soul no less. Thou art *Loves* Victim;
　　and must dye a death more mysticall and *high*

"a *death,* in which who *dyes* Loves his *death,*
　　and dyes againe, and would for ever so be slaine!

"And that there be Fit executioners for thee
　　Ripe men of Martyrdome who bidd thee come

"and write thy spouses radiant *Name* upon
　　thy triumphant brows, thy weake brest.

"Blest powers forbid thy tinder life,
　　Should bleed upon a barbarous Knife;

"Or some base hand have power to race
    Thy Brest's soft cabinet, and uncase

"soules so sweet. Each heav'nly word
    Shall flourish on thy browes Sparkling

"with the sacred flames, Of a thousand soules.
    Thousands of crown'd soules throng to bee

"Themselves thy *crowne*. Thy Wounds shall blush
    to such bright scars, And thy old woes shall now

"smile on thee, All thy sorrows here
    shall shine, And thy suff'rings be divine

"So Kisse the sweetly-killing Dart and teach thy lips
    heav'n with those *delicious wounds* that *weepe*."

Chorus

Athens must have a port in order to survive (to trade and to launch warships), but in order to be Athens, it has to pretend that its port is inessential or inexistent. Piraeus is neither fully inside nor fully outside the city-state. Similarly, masculinity must have an outside that is more intimate than femininity, there must be a part of brotherhood that takes on the burden of contact with the feminine so that masculinity can distinguish itself as such, an immasculinity that is more intimate to masculinity than masculinity itself.

The fag is the limit case for masculinity; it is what remains within the domain of masculinity only to the extent that it is barred from claiming any right to the category. That masculinity is ultimately secured purely through the antagonism of a scapegoat or *pharmakos* (i.e., the fag) tells us something about the nature of masculinity. It is the name of pure violent reaction. A boy will call another boy "fag," not to point out the object choice of his desire for ridicule but to signal to the other boy that what he is doing, saying, wearing, or interested in is not masculine. The reward for calling another boy a "fag" is that one's masculinity is thereby more secured. The anxiety around the status of one's masculinity derives from the emptiness of the category itself. The only definite characteristic of masculinity is a kind of *savoir faire* for nominating fags. But that know-how is nothing more than pure will. Of course, it requires some aptitude for reading the situation in order to make reliable nominations, but ultimately its basis is the unmotivated will to exclusion to the point that a definitive masculinity would be total negativity.

The fag is often given little choice but to accept his fate. But without any other available community of support than the brotherhood in which they function in an abject role, these fags can only attempt to access masculinity through a forcible and often fatal assumption. And it is at this point that they transition into homicidal geeks.

While the homicidal geek's motivation is often a sense of romantic or sexual entitlement, this is not the structure of his destiny. The only avenue apparent for straight, middle-class, suburban fags like Klebold and Rodger, is to pretend to be men, to forcefully and fatally assume the masculine function of pure violence without the goal of attaining social stature which tempers how jocks, whom both Klebold and Rodger single out as antagonists, deploy the same violence. Without the promise of some relatively secure position within the monoculture of high school, the fag accesses the violence of masculinity as pure and unconditional. Thus the violence he deploys is a total violence.

Of course, his act of retribution (and it is always singular) is not 'objectively' total (his 'blaze of glory' must be so terribly unsatisfying), and so it becomes the final, incontrovertible proof of his impotence. The character of Tetsuo from *Akira* is a good example of the fag, and so is the figure of the Sorcerer's Apprentice, and each depicts how the fag's inability to control the violence of the masculinity he so desperately seeks only adds to his humiliation. And yet, for this very reason, the violence deployed by the homicidal fag is masculinity in its total form. The apotheosis of masculinity is not found in the jock or the bro but instead in the homicidal geek, who by pretending to be a man, paradoxically becomes the very model of manliness. Of course, not every fag becomes a homicidal maniac—some become poets.

What masculinity polices with the nomination of the fag is not a set of qualities, the qualities that make a man (e.g., honor, confidence, strength) are alibis. What masculinity polices is the right to police. What men police by the nomination of the fag is the purity of the category of masculinity, which is why men are so fucking boring. The qualities associated with masculinity are historical accidents; what is constant is unconditional violence. *Thumos* has all the discrimination of transcendental reason with none of its prudence.

VI.

As if coming across bootprints in the ash
    of the village I just torched or returning

to the cell only to find a fresh set of bloody
    bootprints leading away from it, I fear word

of my hypostasis precedes me and like
    a hard mark I follow, knowing full well, "what

"error leads must err." And so led would I've
    loved to've left the OC if only to be beloved

of all the brides in Wichita City, and finally squad-bound
    to feel against my cheek the last spasm of the grand

Ismenian dragon as it shoots thru the muscle:
    a crackling around the eyeballs of a sensitive

yellow boy by a muddy wall. But the goddess
    ISIS, friend of slaves and sinners, fearing

for my beloved Ianthe's sanity, dicked me
    out of my clam chowder and strapped me

with a luciferous beard of glued pubes,
    forcing me at gunpoint to git 'er done.

It just drives home that each dong's a consolation,
    consigliere to an eight-fingered duke

decreeing everything come in twos,
    and even that what straddles proves

the rule, scant choice flesh-replacement
    that mendeth not for my poor cunt.

"Unhappyie me, I say, and wilt not stand?
    Com, let me rubb and chafe it with my hand!

"Look, he but stands as stiff as he were made of steele,
    And plays at peacock twixt my Leggs right blythe."

With this, I, Iphys, an accidental merkin,
    must rummage night after night, tart after tart,

on Pompey's Élysées, looking for expiation
    and finding instead a lost troop of what few

hundredths limped away from the sanguine champs
    who remain bleached by sun and memory.

I watch them as they slowly sort themselves into
    the various Elysian shake junts jotting the bulwarks,

where pastie-pasted epigones grease poles
    under black light (evidence of things unseen).

Alone, I do not ramble on like some boulevardier,
    but neither do I dawdle in the doorway like some crusty Eros.

I blithesomely pursue. I stuff the whole thing in my mouth.
    With baited breath I wait to stuff my wad in the Tethyan delta,

hoping it might catch on, I might schwing
    as my nails graze a razed Olympus Mons.

Knowingly, her whispering eye winks between scissoring
    hams or shakes with disdain beneath a furrowed wag.

It complements my implement, knowing full well I
    can't pop and lock harnessed to a goddess's *oblige*.

Regardless, my eyes follow its widening gyre
    from behind as it descends toward the stage;

she pops her trunk to reveal the once-reviled
    brown eye blue suddenly unrivaled, through which

I can see the human remains in this ballerina.
    The old Iphys would've discouraged such a display.

But me, bone-in chicken, I do it anyway,
    and not for myself, nor for this Bolshoi in boyshorts

but for them that's got the say-so, waving Kraft Singles
    advanced on the ides against that Gipper Gruyère, slim

cheese on discharge, them that's got the shakes so bad
    the stripper stands still, their bodies shipped home

in Ziplocks stuffed with pills but hearts and minds
    back in Djerba, fat on the fruit from the tree of knowledge.

Here, their eyes follow this tiny fragile human body
    darting across a no-man's-land to the sound of "Bombs

over Baghdad," the assiest *esse est percipi.* Her struggle
    makes her tits shake. Her repudiation twerks.

Retreating, she offers a flank here, a teat there;
    her shanks scissor; her rump shakes.

The dance is her escape, the pole, a rope tossed down.
    She is passed man to man, uncollectible ransom.

One after the other, in turn we approach
    the murderous angel to pay homage and see

how close we can get and not be destroyed,
    how much juice we can come away with. And so,

when my turn comes I do not hesitate. And Thomas-like,
    I reach my trembling hand toward the proffered wound,

tuck in a twice folded buck, and come away unscathed,
    except for the mark that I make in the minds of these men:

the cheesy discharge and the limp legionnaire,
    the romantic recruit storming castles in air,

the field medic nursing a beer in the back,
    the grunt having waitresses try on his flak,

the sore-felt shore left and shanghaied ex-felchers,
    the salt-cod peacekeepers and brackish-brew belchers,

the gang pressed and planked; the Academi mercs,
    les mariners anciens and mechanical turks,

the war-rape regaler recounting a spoil
    to ballerinas trying not to recoil,

the few, the proud, the many defectors,
    traitors, eighty-sixers, and blitzed sixty-eighters,

the queer sailor preening his drunk none-the-wiser,
    the lap-danced jarhead, skivvies soaked from a geyser,

grabby guerrilla unceremoniously
    bounced, the MP thrusting his dollar thusly.

From gob-eyed swab to salty seafarer,
    from indignant conscript to war-tested elder,

from Notium, Gettysburg, Hastings, Korea,
    from verdure Verdun and sandy Fallujah,

each is the center of this universe
    of starry eyes, held there by the insistence

to be this very thing or nothing at all.
    (And since anything perforce prefers to be

rather than not to be, one happens to be
    exactly that which was anticipated, as if

salvaged from the void. And so this ham-fisted
    tip is legal tender in a lingua franca that sounds

from pay to play, from fat stacks to stacked fatties,
    any alternative being interdict: idiolect or cant.

Nothing I touch will finally break.
    Even this elastic crêpe my tip deforms

snaps back in place, creasing the clams that grease her,
    garter pressing to her oily thickness

the slough of my stack straight from the FedEx,
    the slice of my bread fresh out the food dispenser.

But if I thumb mine own depths, do I come
    out intact? Or am I just a fool for love, aloof

for the rough trade, sap for the *pas seul*?
    A loose pidgin or screwless tool? A sad-sack

sans chat? A cashless lass lashed and strapped
    to a plummeting daisycutter shrieking? A collar

ringed or a rung angelus, snookered, and had
    over a barrel by the herald archangel? Or am I up

shit's creek with a buttload of petals,
    a barrel of monkeys, and a laurel of gaffs?

Am I a man promising happiness to end all happinesses?
    Or am I a falsie, a false flag, a fag selfie?

Crudely were we fucked by those
    who had a gas saluting us.

Even as our lines were broken
    and hearing our kooky camp canticles,

holy Socrates called us faggots from heaven,
    appropriate sobriquet seeing as we

were those penetrated and thus lacking worth,
    outlawed and unmanned and effeminate cowards

preferring a coward's life of shame in Plato's Closet
    to the glorious and blessed death of a hero.

But since they cannot physically
    transform us cowardly men with our

female love of penetration,
    into the women we by nature are,

the punishment will be the closest
    possible approximation

to such a correct penalty:
    They will make us spend the rest of

our lives in utter precarity, forever
    conscripts in combat positions.

We were sent to the ends of the earth in search
    of a body or a soma, a physis or compounded interest,

and where the known world ended
    there was more world and the same.

There was no threshold we passed
    or through which we might return.

I tried so hard to break, but as part of this world
    without end, I too, like the yew, bent and did not break.

We tore the fair fruit and stripped its leaves and knew
    no more moral discrimination; the petals of this flower

made us to forget that mortal taste
    that brought death into the world,

and so we found there a kind of Eden and an innocence,
    which we were more than reluctant to leave.

And though we wept bitterly, we were forced
    back to the ships and tied fast to the benches.

The others got on board, took to their places,
    and smote the grey sea with their oars.

But it was too late, we'd seen the end of the world,
    and no Lethean cocktail would make us forget it.

For us, the epic, stretched to its limit, literally shot
    through with the indifferent figures that it braids

within the interval of its recitation, passes into nonsense,
    becomes a ravenous speech that mocks the lure of reality,

the homecoming of meaning at the end of a tour
    punctuated by the hollow rap of far-off fire.

Home, the war-poem doesn't stop writing itself.
    Its filibuster delays finally the answer to what

sounded like a question but was just a tree
    falling into the abyss at the core of the heart

of the void of its nothingness: a fantasy on blank,
    the coming kingdom where I blew all them hadjis.

Slowly each layer is stripped, even the lace-like skin.
    The suspense kills, and our anticipation articulates

the function of the beautiful, luring us close
    to that for which there is no substitute,

without exposing us to the horror of its ill fit.
    Too-big a caliber of silver bullet, a saber

rattling in someone else's scabbard, an unwieldy strap,
    a prosthetic third leg or an untrimmed maypole,

a loose-fitting blackjack or baggy cheek slapper,
    a sock and rough skin or half-baked po'taster,

turkey stuffing and giblet gravy with beer-battered
    bear bait, or a tackle-box's seven-inch Finicky Tickler,

an insert, a supplement, or pullout in Sunday's rag,
    a loose cannon; a busted nut and stripped bolt,

a jury-rigged jib or jittery nib, dad's date in need
    of a new notch, honkey two-step, donkey shame,

a trusty sick shooter, a rusty rump-roasting spit,
    or spit-shined strappy stainless-steel stiletto,

Jared Leto's mic, Mike Tyson's Jell-O mold,
    or Tyson's O'Hara's Leda's swan's liver served cold.

Thus home is exactly how we left it,
    only everything now out of place just so,

each word slightly more or less
    than the space it makes in air, its sound

scraping the hollow from the inside, tongue still
    not grown accustomed to its taste. So grown

ever watchful, even here, in the club,
    careless in our need to be seen watching.

She sees us watching her, but we do not look to see,
    and so unentwined, the unevenness of our social

relation is work, is the noncoincidence that gives
    myself to me, and is the engine that exchanges now

and then. What man does she see in this limp sleeve
    pinned to itself, pant leg knotted or eerily unfilled?

I am no more or less slapped back together
    than the others here, each having left a piece roadside,

and yet even the intimacy of having swapped
    every body part with every other yet cannot

overcome the distance I nurture in place of a self,
    coming from the desert storm where I maxed man,

became at most no man to a hair's breadth of the No
    One, hole encompassing both threat and hearth,

its thickless rim what remains to be
    of fullest negation for it to be and remain as such.

In this I went furthest, outdoing even God
    (whose crawlspace is our earth),

going so far as to destroy all evidence,
    not by torching corpses or leveling dwellings,

but by never having committed the crime
    in the first place (such that even Jesus greens).

In this did I rip the sanctum's seam to see
    that God's corpse is his own empty throne.

When not a drop of blood more
    could be wrung out of the universe,

the negation of man immediately transformed into
    its opposite: the absolute coming-to-be of this

one man that I am, not in order to carry
    the sentence for such a crime but to receive

grace in the form of an infernal
    repetition of a now-lost privatization,

incessantly to reenact the aborted birth of this
    reality to keep the *anamnesis* of its true foreclosure

from collapsing the lapse in which we go about our days
    in the innocence of our never having needed to have been.

What figure do we cut, this forlorn troop,
    whose commonwealth is absolute privation?

What municipality is perched upon this duty
    only to capricious instantiating violence?

We belong to this life to the extent that our negation
    of it, or rather our testimony as to what about it

persists in negation, affirms that which is as
    the brutal installation of what just happens to be.

I was blessed to remain as the very figure
    of self-annihilation, like an unpainted corner

hidden under a pile of ash. I carried with me
    the voided transaction of the universe as a stack

of ones, which I keep trying to pawn off onto
    this stripper—desiring no longer to be held together

by catapres and by the unwavering surveillance
    of corn-fed flag-wavers just so I'll salute from the back

of a deuce and a half twice a year—but her garter
    can only fit so much, and I'm running a surplus

of that which is and should not be.) As her song
    begins its interminable (if only!) crescendo,

her hocks hiked, heels over head, she spreads
        her phalanxes into a V sign to prove that she too

is pink on the inside, that her heart
        was shipped home in a biohazard bag,

that on the roadside, near the meeting of the waters,
        she too felt earth tremble from her entrails.

And at the moment of the big reveal,
        when I would have preferred a merciful curtain

or a dead blackout, she arches her back
        and, prodded by a *fer chrissake!* ejaculated

from a dark booth in the back,
        drives the two long spikes of her heels

into the boards on either side of her
        and peels her back end up off the stage.

Chorus

If this poem is about anything, it is about the horror of brotherhood, the community of pure expulsion to which no one belongs and for which the author's every word, against his will, is an apology. How then to begin to learn how no longer to speak in its name? How to withdraw from its speaking position without thereby assuming its privilege? How to escape from a community to which no one belongs but in which one is always included, an abdication that carries the weight of sovereignty? It is here, at the point of articulation of an impossible disavowal, that the issue of the pink of his dick becomes not only an issue of language but of poetry, of the poetic register of language. At the point where language seeks to silence itself as such, at the point where language seems to touch its illegible outside, there appears the fullness of its presence, the perfection of its awful significance, because at the very edge of language is not its pure and noble ideal but instead the police. He writes as if to exit a brotherhood that has already expelled him and whose edict of expulsion brings him immediately into its dominion.

The *pharmakos* (also *pharmakon*) was a person from within the community of Ancient Athens who was forced to be the symbolic bearer of the impurities of the city. Often nominated in pairs (a man and a woman), they were expelled from the city, whipped with fig branches (they were also called *kradisites*, the "man/woman of the fig tree," or *sykobakkhos*, "Bacchus of the fig"), and stoned. While not always killed, the *pharmakos* was certainly tortured or exiled as a form of civic expiation and purification. The *pharmakos* is the name for what the law covers but does not protect, that which the law touches only to the extent that revokes any rights. Interestingly, the *pharmakos* was often disabled, 'marked' in some way. Aesop, who Achilles' people forced off a cliff, is traditionally depicted as disfigured. Silver-tongued Thersites, who defied Agamemnon and whom Achilles murders, was, like Aesop, called, "very ugly," and was most likely deformed. An Ancient iambic poet and exile who sometimes depicted himself in poems as a *pharmakos* (in one, a woman thrashes his testicles with a fig branch as if he were a scapegoat—

132

though this may have been a treatment for impotence), Hipponax, called a "certain deformed poet" (*Hipponactem quendam poetam deformem*), is said to have been "despised for his deformity" (*pro deformitate contemptus est*) and to have had a "hideous and defective face" (*foeda et vitiosa facie*). His poems present us with the earliest extant depictions of the pharmakos rite.

The point of all this hack scholarship on the *pharmakos* comes down to the need to formalize how the core values of the dominant culture in the U.S. are secured by a violence that functions to deter any representations of the injustice inherent in the culture or, failing that, to eradicate the source of such representations. The major scapegoats paraded out by this culture are clear to anyone with the slightest detachment from it. The point of linking the figure of the fag to that of the *pharmakos* is to suggest that this violence has a name, "masculinity." Neither a set of criteria for membership nor an inherent privilege of a biological crapshoot, masculinity is essentially the illegitimate and violent expulsion of what is not masculine and nothing more. The concept has no positive content. It is pure war, and poetry's two perennial themes are love and war.

Thus the poem's introduction of the figure of the veteran, who performs masculinity in the field and in the strip club as the obverse of the fag and is representative of how masculinity transcends the man, that is, how the perfection of masculine violence leaves as its remnant the shattered body and mind of the veteran. The soldier does not succeed in war but is consumed along with every other resource at hand, human and otherwise. The coincidence of a human being with masculine violence sublates into a perfection of masculinity in the form of its precipitate—masculinity fully realized in the emasculation of the vet. It is the vet who has witnessed the sheen of civilization shimmer with the horror that shallowly subtends it. What honor is there in defending a nation which is little more than the violence one immediately deploys in its service? And against what? Infinitely exchangeable variations on the same constitutive cruelty? The lessor of all evils?

To see the vet as anything but the residual smear of this violence is to look on them with contempt. To consider the veteran as an inhuman stain is coincident with one's care for the vet, for contempt for the vet is exactly the invisibility conferred on them by the state, which so efficiently discards them. To stare at the human wreck that is the vet, to take one's fill of the fair sight, is immediately to negate the paternalistic commemoration that absolves the state of the crime that it simply is. Like Actaeon, witness to the all-too-human nudity of the goddess Artemis and thus rendered mute and told "to tell them if you can," the vet is unable to bear witness to the transgression of all limits that constitutes state power. It is the body of the vet which testifies to the totality and the everydayness of this violence and also the institutional power mobilized to explain away the wretchedness that this body indicates, orienting it through strategic neglect toward the anodynes that will inevitably have the vet panting once more for that taste of lotus blossoms bursting from the tip of their service pistol.

VII.

The unblinking spotlight reflected her pronounced
    eye in our eye, a sorrowful braid of our eye-beams.

Then through a slit in the curtain, the peeler peeled
    out, so we took her cue and poured out ourselves,

avoiding each other's gazes, a lick of fire
    in everyone's head, each muttering incomprehensibly

to himself. That was my last night on base.
    I awoke the following morning, gathered my things

and made my way to canteen. As I enjoyed
    my exquisite meal, I took in the scenery around me:

the perfectly built architecture of the building, the pretty
    flowers in the gardens, the luxurious furniture and décor,

the cascading fountains. I reached up to my neck
    to feel my special necklace, and I felt nothing there.

It was truly over, confirmed by the ticket I held.
    At the airport, I smoked in the designated area.

I checked the standby list, but before I could speak
    to the person behind the ticket counter,

a man clasped my shoulder and thrust at me
    his first-class ticket. A woman (his wife, I assumed)

hugged me. The tears that rippled in her eyes
    were nothing more than the dolorous drool

of the newly orphaned or the last globule
      of jism forming at the meatus of a soldier's

softening prick, which he wipes on the candy-striped
      rag he's conjured abracadabra-like from the *kiss al-fatat*.

I boarded. And just as the night about the moon grew
      gray, one wing leaned westward to the fading rose.

I took delight in sipping the wine that was served
      while I enjoyed the relaxing journey.

In my *jahiliyya* days, I never thought twice
      about flying. But that was long before

I'd had AA fire spin me out of a Huey or seen
      Scylla's spawn spew from her screeching urethra.

Alone among these travelers, I did not barrel
      into their shared and venal future. The future

takes forever. In place of its ordained realization,
      we can't help but wish for a nowhere, those of us

who've imbibed on that fair fruit, or wish to end it,
      wish to turn the world into what it already is,

a gorgeous and desperate carnality barely
      outrunning the very charnel that fuels it,

an anomaly beatified purely by its improbability:
      the survivor's merit, the unelected *pharmakon's* conceit.

For those of us who return, our very survival
      is refutation. The guns are the colors. Before long,

ISIS will have us tonguing the jeweless setting
    of the polymastic light-bearer's crenelated crown.

Virgin ISIS, crystal whose absolute clarity
    is composed of infinite refractions, have mercy

on frustrated hunters such as we, forbidden to fire friendily.
    Grant us immunity. There's always sand in my Big Mac.

It appears, so-great Socrates, you disappointment
    to a virgin's bricklayer and a hysterical temptress,

that the computer has annihilated the number three,
    and widows don their creditor's panoply,

and by saving the life of the coward Alcibiades,
    you secured your passage at the hands of the Thirty.

I ain't got nothing to offer you, and so, *Tort N'avetz,*
    my funny *philosophe,* how do you take it?

Cause I'll happily hang on to my bony *aulos*
    until you've become but a faint *eidos.* My lips

do taste the bitter reed they wet withal. My purity
    a casualty of whatever instrument I now tongue.

May this music soften me, but a dying thrall,
    and divest me for good of this my peg and awl.

Its wah and its chooglin' bass never reach you
    in your *topos koinos,* but they move my Virgil

(a batonless bobby) and me blittering across
    the Gorgon Stare, *immunis sedens aliena ad pabula*

("the decommed KillerBee sucks on the rich's
        booty"), two ravers, two unequal weapons

in an equally unequal throng, a bar
        without poles, a club without cop,

where closet dramas go unstaged
        even though the stage remains, vacant

and lit by neon flashing the idiom, "This Is It."
        That vacancy is not what is other to our being

here but what exists of the difference between
        our absence and the difference between

our absence and our presence. The idiom
        is its own and marks the void of any order.

And so with nothing left to say, I'll end on a quote.
        A poet once wrote, "There's no such thing

as a breakdown," but I think he meant
        to say, "You can't say it that way anymore."

Or is it the other way around? Oh,
        what do I care? The poets are all liars.

And besides, the lyres are all broken. And Ianthe
        yet a kissless virgin. Her steps in the ash read,

"*November Mike Tango*, for Caesar's I am,
        and wild for to hold though I seem tame."

Afterword

Dear Lawrence ~ Reading yr psychotic book, I swear I feel "ting'd with a resplendent glow," which is what Keats wrote of Byron's verse when he compared it to a moon-soaked cloud. Were I not so shy, I'd say that reading yr lines makes me something of a masturbator, at least in Byron's estimation of Keats—by which I mean yr estimation of me—whose lines were to him nothing but the "outstretched poesy of a miserable Self-polluter," an epithet meant to capture what's most offensive in *Endymion*, I suppose, like "the onanism of poetry" whose pleasures are the effect of *hard fucking work*, each line "extracted out of being suspended daily by a street walker." I'm not sure what you saw on first looking into my porn, but I can't help but wonder whether I've offended you similarly? Is that why y've made me yr whore? In any case, you seem to want it both ways as you suck yr lines from my marrow while indulging the fantasy of being strung-up yrself. I'm just trying to understand yr spirit-slurry, which y've excreted like some kind of truth ~~semen~~ serum and by whose language y've chastely concealed yr boner. I mean, if you really want to be a porn star, no need to blow my cock in public. As if I'd seized a body to plunder for my pleasure while ventriloquizing yr own meek speech in advance, singing "Yes, yes, fuck me harder!" Come out, come out, dear Lawrence, and kiss me like a man. No one's come closer to realizing the poem as universal expression than I have. So sing yr crotch-rot to yrself, or shut yr face. No need to default to a chaste performance of holding-back. I'd be yr power bottom, if y'd only ask. Just wipe yr own cum, whose spirit's no bone but a hole, not an abstract ghost, but the thing itself. If y'd only bother to think like a dialectician for a minute, rather than a sloppy *eromenos* trying to climb up from under some imaginary corpse, y'd let go of me and let yr poem breathe. If I can teach you anything, it's that porn abstracts nothing, cuz it's the material residue of a systematic abstraction that conditions yr fucking poem, too. So who's turning whose labor into jargon?

The whole point is that that the militarization of our life world is already the realization of the market's aestheticization, which makes your lines totally redundant. Haven't you read your own fucking palm, for Chrissakes? I mean, the autonomy of yr poem is adjunct to that of a Kalashnikov, unlike the glory hole I've turned into an alter of purest devotion. Talk about pretentious disclosures! Just remove all yr clothes for us to better feign yr own sub-prole orgy. Did you write this poem in a cave or a closet? Seriously, though, I love you and yr poem. Thanx for showing me a thing or two, and for returning the total form of my body to me, or at least my strap-on and my beard. I'll no longer look for utopia in a piece of military hardware, but in yr own pink welt of origin as I kiss yr puckered star. —*Rob Halpern*

Notes

"Muse So Gray" is composed almost entirely of text from Patricia Churchland's *Neurophilosophy*.

"The Warlord Patroclus Addressing His Slave Girl, Iphys" sprung fully formed from my head and is dedicated to my friend Lauren.

"And Others Who Are Mute Auditors" is a heavily revised version of a poem of the same name first published in *Sorites* (Tea Party Republicans Press, 2011). The poem is a writing-through (whatever that means) of Plato's *Republic* (section V is composed only of lines taken from the book). The "poet-assassin of León" mentioned in section IX is Rigoberto López Pérez, a Nicaraguan poet and composer who assassinated the dictator Anastasio Somoza Garcia. The final section, "XII. Epilogue," comprises quotes from Plato, Philip K. Dick, and Jacques Lacan.

"Iphys's Physis" was written mainly with the aid of urbandictionary.com, a stellar website with a problematic name, and Wikipedia, which is considered a somewhat more serious resource, and began as a meditation on the coupling of violence and sexuality in the disciplining of straight masculine subjects as depicted in Warren G and Nate Dogg's single "Regulate." The rest of the poem is sprinkled with quotations from "The Choise of Valentines Or the Merie Ballad of Nash His Dildo," some Genet from *Funeral Rites,* Donne, Virgil, HD, Catullus, Milton, Chaucer and some Shakespeare, Lord Byron, Ovid, Ginsberg, and others I've happily forgotten. Many of the quoted lines in the dedication are from Halpern's *Music for Porn.* Telemachus's dialogue in section III is almost totally collaged from Elliot Rodger's manifesto, *My Twisted World,* though the passage, "My misogyny is [. . .] power to hurt women," is from a Tumblr post, I think, by the writer Jimmy Chen, who curiously still refers to it as *his* misogyny. Patroclus's speech that follows is a partially edited homophonic translation of the first few pages of Frank Stanford's "Battlefield Where the Moon Says I Love You," using an exaggerated Southern accent. The setting of Stanford's poem is near the town where I'm from, so it's the most personal section of the poem. Isis's address to Ianthe at the end of section V is collaged from Richard Crashaw's "Hymn to Saint Teresa." Some of Rodger's language reappears near the end of the poem, when Iphys is returning home from war. The poem is dedicated, of course, to Rob, whose first book woke me from my dogmatic slumbers and at whose house this *bête immonde petit monde* was first trotted out.

I want to thank Josef Kaplan and Douglas Piccinnini for publishing the earlier version of "And Others" in *Sorites*. Additionally, I must thank Chris Catanese for conversation and encouragement during the composition of "Iphys's Physis." Also, thanks to Brandon Brown and Marie Buck for their generous comments on the manuscript when it was in its early stages, to Laura Mauldin, who Beckett-like convinced me to go on when I couldn't go on, and to James Sherry for patiently and thoroughly poring over several more drafts of this book than he probably had wanted.

ROOF BOOKS
the best in language since 1976

Recent & Selected Titles

- PARSIVAL by Steve McCaffery. 88 p. $15.95
- DEAD LETTER by Jocelyn Saidenberg. 94 p. $15.95
- social patience by David Brazil. 136 p. $15.95
- THE PHOTOGRAPHER by Ariel Goldberg. 84 p. $15.95
- TOP 40 by Brandon Brown. 138 p. $15.95
- DEAD LETTER by Jocelyn Saidenberg. 98 p. $15.95
- THE MEDEAD by Fiona Templeton. 314 p. $19.95
- LYRIC SEXOLOGY VOL. 1 by Trish Salah. 138 p. $15.95
- INSTANT CLASSIC by erica kaufman 90 p. $14.95
- A MAMMAL OF STYLE by Kit Robinson
  & Ted Greenwald. 96 p. $14.95
- VILE LILT by Nada Gordon. 114 p. $14.95
- DEAR ALL by Michael Gottlieb. 94 p. $14.95
- FLOWERING MALL by Brandon Brown. 112 p. $14.95.
- MOTES by Craig Dworkin. 88 p. $14.95
- APOCALYPSO by Evelyn Reilly. 112 p. $14.95
- BOTH POEMS by Anne Tardos. 112 p. $14.95

Roof Books are published by
Segue Foundation
300 Bowery • New York, NY 10012
For a complete list, please visit **roofbooks.com**

Roof Books are distributed by
SMALL PRESS DISTRIBUTION
1341 Seventh Street • Berkeley, CA. 94710-1403.
spdbooks.org